How Do You Tell a Hungry Soul She Cannot Have a Bible?

and Other Stories from
United Pentecostal Church Missionaries

Compiled and edited by
Dorsey L. Burk

Copyright 1998
Foreign Missions Division
United Pentecostal Church International
8855 Dunn Road
Hazelwood, Missouri 63042-2299

Contents

Africa

1. Ghana: Evangelism by Dead Men — 7
   by James Poitras
2. Kenya: A Blessing to the Heart — 13
   by Patricia Hall
3. Tanzania: Stuck! — 21
   by Pamela Smoak
4. Uganda: Deliverance from Death in Rwanda — 25
   by Darline Royer

Asia

5. India: The Story of Mala Baral of India — 33
   by Stanley Scism
6. Taiwan: "The Unknown God" Found — 37
   in a Heathen Temple by Tom Bracken

Europe/Middle East

7. Bulgaria: How Do You Tell a Hungry Soul She — 45
   Cannot Have a Bible? by Evangeline Rodenbush
8. Eastern Europe: Stories of Eastern Europe — 49
   by Cheryl Craft
9. Germany: "I'll Praise Him" — 53
   by Bev Burk
10. Russia: The St. Petersburg Revival — 63
    by William Turner

Pacific

11. Indonesia: The Kang Family Story — 69
    by Helen White
12. New Zealand: Of Fleas and Miracles — 73
    by Judy Addington
13. Papua New Guinea: Halu Village Glorifies God — 77
    by Esther Henry

14. Philippines: Saved by Superstition   81
    by Cecil Sullivan
15. Tonga: Our Great Welcome to the Kingdom of Tonga 91
    by Bennie Blunt

South America

16. Brazil: "Only You, Lord"   95
    by Bennie DeMerchant
17. Brazil: In Deep Water   103
    by Theresa DeMerchant
18. Ecuador: Protected by Angels   109
    by Stuart Lassetter
19. Venezuela: Juana Garcia of Caracas   113
    by James Burton

Deputational Travel

20. Flying High on Deputation   119
    by Bennie Blunt

Miscellaneous

21. Recapping the Rash Story in Missions   121
    by Carol Rash

Faith Promise

22. Laborers Together with God   125
    by J. S. Leaman

Preface

One of my earliest memories is of large snakeskins draped over the mahogany banister at the old church in South Modesto, California. I was just a small lad, but the skins brought to the church by Brother and Sister Holms, missionaries to Liberia, made a lasting impression on me. For me they symbolized the sacrifice and dedication the missionaries were making to preach the gospel.

As the years went by, other missionaries filled our pulpit and moved me with their stories. Their tales of deliverance, healing, protection, salvation, and trusting God encouraged and challenged me. It was like hearing a continuation of the Book of Acts. Instead of Peter and Paul, the names included Ellis and Marjorie Scism, Bill and Mollie Thompson, Lewis and Sally Morley, Lucille Farmer, E. L. and Nona Freeman, and many more.

A new generation of missionaries is now on the front lines. I find their stories just as exciting and challenging. In the following pages you will have the opportunity to read twenty-two stories, primarily written by missionaries currently under appointment by the United Pentecostal Church International. Weep and rejoice with us and let God speak to your heart as you read *How Do You Tell a Hungry Soul She Cannot Have a Bible?*

Dorsey L. Burk

Chapter 1

Evangelism by Dead Men

by **James Poitras**, Ghana

In a little more than two and one-half years 5,901 people have received the Holy Ghost in Ghana, West Africa. Ghanaians take every opportunity to preach the gospel. The gospel is preached on buses, in prisons, under trees, in places of business, and any other place where people may gather.

Kissing the bride at a wedding is usually set aside for the honeymoon evening, and the gospel is preached even in the wedding service. The next morning the entire bridal party, family members, and well wishers are back in church for a thanksgiving service. At naming ceremonies and baby dedications, the gospel is unfolded. However, of all the places where the gospel is exposed to hungry hearts, none seem to have as a great an impact as the funeral activities.

Life in Ghana stops for a funeral. Work ceases. Offices close. Vendors pack away their market goods. All scheduled activities are put aside. When a good person dies, the whole town turns out for the funeral. At the funeral of a good person it is often exclaimed, "The town has turned upside down." Seldom are birthdays celebrated, but the day a person dies is of great importance and is always remembered.

The Ghanaian culture puts much emphasis on the manner in which a funeral is observed. A "bad" funeral is a disgrace, and a "good" one is considered to be very respectful to the memory of the deceased. Everybody speaks about the funeral long after it has been observed.

The entire area will show up for the wake keeping, usually held all night with two to three preachers ministering. The burial follows on the next morning with everyone reminded of the brevity of life. The next day the friends and family of the deceased are back in church again for the memorial service.

The funeral is perhaps the most dramatic event in the town. There is wailing, singing, and dancing. After the service everyone walks from the church to the cemetery, even if it is on the other side of town. The funeral could be weeks and even months after the actual death of a person. (In such delays, the body is frozen.) Much time, planning, and money must be expended to make sure the funeral is a befitting one. Men wear the "cloth" in the form of a toga, and all clothing worn is usually either red or black, considered the mourning or funeral colors.

In this funeral setting we have the remarkable stories of two young Ghanaian men. Each one, at different times and locations, was snatched by death in the prime of life. Their stories represent a most effective means of evangelism, one never recorded in the Book of Acts. It is evangelism by a dead man!

Pastor Edwudzie Sampson, a tremendous church planter in Ghana, takes care of seven churches and serves as their pastor. In 1990 he began the groundwork for a church at Winneba, a university town in the Central Region.

A sister had returned from Liberia and was living in Winneba. Converts from Winneba were coming to church at Awutu, several miles away. The wife of a Muslim chief was converted, which caused no small stir. Then a young man named James Bernard Ghartey and his wife were baptized and, together with his mother, Madam Araba Mansah, started attending the Awutu church.

Three weeks after arriving in Ghana I visited Awutu United Pentecostal Church for my first time. James, his wife, and his mother received the Holy Spirit that morning, along with two other local people. With that, a decision was made to start a church at Winneba.

The first church service was held on Sunday, March 27, 1995. There were five adults and three children in service. On April 3 Brother Ghartey told the pastor that by December of that year the Winneba church would reach one hundred in attendance. Four days later Brother Ghartey passed away.

The funeral activities took place on April 21-23, 1995. What Brother Ghartey said came to pass, because of the evangelism of a dead man. At his funeral, his testimony was given and the Acts 2:38 message was preached. This message was new to the people of Winneba.

Over 2,000 people attended the wake keeping alone. Many began to register their names to join the church or to know more about what we believe. In the next few months thirty-nine people were baptized in Jesus' name and thirty-five received the Holy Ghost. Four of Brother Ghartey's family members now attend the church at Winneba. One of his brothers is now preaching the gospel. More than one hundred people have been baptized, and the church attendance is regularly above eighty people.

Just several months after our arrival in Ghana, we attended a service at Labadi United Pentecostal Church. Brother Craig Sully, a fellow missionary in West Africa, was visiting us, and he preached, with many people receiving the Holy Spirit. One of the young men who received the Spirit was Joseph Okpoti. He had just started attending the church, after being converted from another group that did not have the fullness of truth.

When Joe began attending the United Pentecostal Church, he received criticism from all quarters, including his family and their church. The head pastor of his former church had tried to persuade him to return there, but to no avail. His mother, after realizing that nothing would cause Joe to rescind his decision, finally threatened to disown him.

None of these things moved Joe. He was bold enough to tell them that they needed to join the UPC themselves and learn more about the truth of God's Word. He continued in the church and participated in all the activities. He became a strong tree in the church. Little did anyone realize that this tree was about to fall.

A young man, Joe died a month after receiving the Holy Ghost. During the funeral services Pastor Lartey and his entire church of nearly five hundred members rallied together for the activities.

I was at another church on a Friday night with a visiting American preacher, Brother Theron Smith. As he preached, the Lord impressed upon me that I should immediately go to the wake keeping for this brother after service that night. When I reached the wake keeping there was a wave of surprise among our members to think that their superintendent, who was newly arrived in Ghana, would attend the wake keeping of a new convert.

Joe's former church had also fully attended the activities. There were about twenty-five hundred people scattered anywhere they could find to sit. I was escorted into a small room where Joe, the deceased, was laid out on a bed. Bright lights lit the corpse, robed in white. Women and men kept rushing in, singing songs and dancing.

Because the Labadi church is one church that believes in winning souls at such occasions, they preached the gospel and portrayed their love for God by caring for others. People expressed, "That church really cares about their members." Others said, "There is love in that church!"

When the funeral was over four members of the family had been converted to the United Pentecostal Church. These were Joe's mother, who had stood so strongly against the UPC, his sister, and two brothers. That year alone nearly four hundred people received the Holy Spirit at

Labadi. Some of these were directly due to the evangelism by a dead man.

••

Jim and Linda Poitras, professional educators, met in Nigeria as Associates In Missions, married, and in 1985 received their full missionary appointment. Following a decade in Nigeria, they accepted the challenge to go to Ghana, revive the work, and restore the training program that had been inactive for seven years. Arriving in Ghana in February 1995, Brother Poitras became the field superintendent. He opened ACTS-Ghana (Bible school) and set up a national prayer movement called P. U. S. H. (Pray Until Something Happens) Prayer Ministries. In January 1996 he also became the area coordinator of the English-speaking nations of West Africa. Recently he initiated the Reach Through Teaching Ministries, generating monthly teaching literature for West African pastors and churches. Sister Poitras serves as the national ladies president and an instructor in ACTS-Ghana and teaches their daughters, Melinda and Candra.

Chapter 2

A Blessing to the Heart

by **Patricia Hall**, Kenya

My husband and I returned to Kenya in February 1996 to begin our fourth missionary term in Africa. God has performed many miracles for us in our eighteen years as missionaries, but what happened in 1996 has truly blessed many hearts.

In May of that year, I found myself flying back to the United States. I had promised my three daughters that, if at all possible, I would be there for the birth of their first babies. The due date for Melissa, our youngest daughter, was the middle of May, and God had provided the money for me to make this trip. On May 17, Elizabeth Layne Harris was born. It was special moment and I was thrilled to be a part of it.

For a few months I had been experiencing some chest discomfort, so I made an appointment with a doctor in Arlington, Texas. After I explained some of my symptoms, the doctor booked me for a stress test with a leading cardiologist, Dr. Lenhoff. Elizabeth was five days old when I failed the stress test and the doctor told me that it appeared that my heart had several blockages. My family history was already against me, with my father having had quadruple bypass surgery, my mother having had angioplasty, and my brother dying of massive heart attack at thirty-three years of age. The doctor scheduled an angiogram for the following Tuesday, May 29, 1996.

After talking with our children, I called the secretary of Foreign Missions and requested that my husband, Jim, come back to the United States to be with me. He flew out the next night and arrived in Arlington to find me in the hospital with unstable angina.

Many people around the world were praying and fasting, and I felt assured that God was with me. Brother John Harris told me that in prayer the Lord had spoken to him and that I was going to be okay. Sister Nona Freeman called with a word from the Lord that confirmed this.

The angiogram revealed that I had ninety-five percent blockage in the right coronary artery. Dr. Lenhoff transferred me to Baylor University Hospital in Dallas, where I underwent an atherectomy with a stent implant in the affected artery. When the surgeon, Dr. Anwar, wrote his report, he told my cardiologist that I needed to remain in the United States for six months to a year until my condition stabilized. Jim and I sought the Lord, and we felt God direct us to return to Kenya. Dr. Lenhoff agreed to let me go with the stipulation that I would be monitored in Nairobi by Dr. Silverstein, a cardiologist there.

We arrived back in Nairobi on July 3, 1996. I felt that God had directed me home by providing the money, but I also felt His hand in bringing me back to Kenya. Yes, I really did feel we were in the perfect will of God, but for the next few months I had to fight fear. Fear would grip me when I felt a pain in my chest. Fear was there in the middle of the night as I thought how far I was from the latest medical procedures and facilities if I had a heart attack.

I went through a period of depression as I experienced a vulnerability I had not felt before. Physically I did well at first, but after three months I began experiencing angina when I tried to walk a distance or climb stairs. During this time I continually rebuked the fear and doubt that kept haunting me.

My husband was a wonderful support to me through this trying time. As an added blessing, our son-in-law, Jonathan Harris, came to help us with the Bible school program, which meant that he, Melissa, and three-month-old Elizabeth lived next door. What a great treat for grandparents! As missionaries we long to spend more time with our children and now grandchildren. We were thrilled to have part of our family with us in Kenya. Jonathan did a great job of organizing and instituting a new training program for the Bible school, and it is going well today.

November 26, 1996, found me at Dr. Silverstein's office. He did a six-month stress test. There were definite changes as well as angina. What I had feared seemed to be happening. My husband and I sat in Dr. Silverstein's office and tried to come to grips with what he was telling us. We were both stunned. I remember coming back to the house with a sick feeling of disappointment and apprehension. I prayed and wept, telling the Lord, "I have given You everything. My desires, my children and grandchildren—but most of all I have given You my life. I don't know what else I can give. Is this how our missionary work will end?"

ND to Dr. Silverstein faxed the results of the stress test to the cardiologist in Arlington, Texas. Together they recommended that we return home immediately for another heart catherization. Much soul searching and seeking the God's will began, and a daily part of my life was spent "before the Lord." I listened for His voice as I tried to make sense out of all it.

We had several guests at this time as mini-crusades and leadership seminars were going on. Brother John Arcovio spoke to me that the Lord was not finished with us in East Africa and everything would be all right. As Brother and Sister David Smith, Brother and Sister Joe Harrod, Jon and Melissa, and Jim and I spent one evening in prayer in our living room, I began to feel the peace of God. The churches at home and many family members and friends were with us in prayer. The World Network of Prayer was alerted, and I felt the assurance that God was in control.

I began reading *Surprise Endings* by Ron Mehl. One statement in that book spoke to me: "The servant of the Lord is indestructible until God is finished with him." I felt God was speaking to me, and I was comforted.

The week we left Kenya, the national board was in session for its semiannual board meeting. On the last day of the meeting, I felt to go to them and have them lay hands on me. Jim told them the reason we were going back to the United States. All eleven of them expressed their concern and assured us they would be in much prayer. As they laid hands on me that afternoon and prayed with a mighty voice, I felt the beautiful peace of God sweep over me. Truly the Lord was present.

On the Sunday we were to leave, Jim told the headquarters church that I had to return to the U.S.A. for more tests on my heart. Life Tabernacle Church gathered around me and prayed until the place was shaken. A dear saint whom we call Mama Sarah came to our house and told me the Lord was with me and that I would be all right. She placed her hands on my chest and, as tears streamed down her face, prayed in her Kikuyu language. Before she left, she said, "You will return to Kenya soon."

It was a hard thing to leave Kenya one week before Christmas, especially to leave our daughter and her family there. Christmas is the loneliest time of any missionary term. We had looked forward to spending the holidays with our children. I felt so bad at leaving Jon and Melissa alone in Kenya. However, they both expressed their concern at what could happen to me if I stayed and possibly had a heart attack. They urged us to go at this time.

We arrived back in the United States on December 16, 1996. The next day I was in Dr. Lenhoff's office and was admitted to Baylor University Hospital in Dallas. That same day a heart catherization was performed. During the procedure I was praising and thanking the Lord for His blessings, for His will in our lives, and for being the Master of every situation. Both doctors doing the catherization were Muslims

A Blessing to the Heart

and finally asked me to be quiet as I was disturbing them. I continued praising God but in a whisper.

When the angiogram was finished, Dr. Anwar and his assistant spoke to me. Both doctors were amazed at the findings. The right coronary artery, where they had implanted the stent, was blocked ninety-eight percent. He told me that it was useless to try to reopen it. He called it a "sick artery." However, from the left coronary artery had come three collateral arteries to the right side of the heart, bypassing the sick artery and providing adequate blood and oxygen. There was no heart damage and no sign of a heart attack.

In my medicated state it was hard to grasp all of what he was telling me. Six months before, these "collateral arteries" were not there; now they are. Dr. Anwar looked at me as I lay on the table in the catherization lab and said, "You can go back to Kenya whenever you want to. You will be fine."

When I returned to my room the doctor actually had to draw a diagram of what they were telling me. Finally we realized what they were trying to tell us. I had a triple heart bypass, but no doctor had performed it.

Tears came to our eyes as we realized what God had done for me. We rejoiced at the mercy and blessing of the Lord. Jim and I have tried to get the Jewish cardiologist and the Muslim cardiologist at Baylor to confirm that this is indeed a miracle. The closest they would come to that is to say, "It is a blessing to the heart."

Dr. Lenhoff felt I needed a few weeks of cardiac rehabilitation to strengthen the "new arteries." As I joined a class of heart patients, the doctor asked each one of us to tell why he was in the class. Some said they had had heart attacks. Some had undergone angioplasty. Others had had heart surgery of three, four, and even five bypasses. When it came my turn I said, "I have a triple bypass, but I did not have surgery." It was a great opportunity to tell what God had done for me. Nurses—and even doctors—have told me that it takes years for collateral arteries to develop, and since they were not there six months before, it was a definite miracle.

Soon it was time to return to Kenya. As we prepared to leave Texas, I went to see my Jewish cardiologist in order for him to release me to go back to Africa. He told me he felt I would be fine and that if anyone had to have a blocked artery, I had picked the best possible way to have it! As I started out the door, I looked at him and said, "It is a miracle." He shook his head affirmatively. There was no other answer. God had given me a "blessing to my heart."

I have felt a renewed purpose in my life since we returned to Kenya. The fear and doubt are gone, and I have continually praised the Lord for His mercy to me. The Kenyan church has rejoiced with us at God's healing touch on my heart. I have witnessed to many people about this great miracle, and all have been amazed. What I have received from the Lord has strengthened my resolve that "the servant of the Lord is indestructible until God is finished with him." I know He is not finished with us in Kenya, and every day I try to give Him my best.

In May 1997 I underwent another six-month stress test. Dr. Silverstein told me it was a better reading than the one in November. I do not feel worthy of all the wonderful things God has done for me. For now, I am trying to do all I know to do to be a blessing to other hearts by teaching, training, and being obedient to His will.

A Blessing to the Heart

Jimmy Hall, a former Kansas District secretary, and his wife, Patricia, received their appointment as UPCI missionaries to Liberia in May 1979. In Liberia Brother Hall served as the field superintendent, overseeing the growth and outreach of the UPC of Liberia, and as the president of Maranatha Bible School in Monrovia, the nation's capital.

In 1991 the Foreign Missions Board asked the Halls to assume the field superintendency of Kenya. In this position Brother Hall is the chief administrative officer of the UPC of Kenya. He also teaches at Life Tabernacle Bible School in Nairobi and oversees the development of the United Pentecostal Church in neighboring Rwanda and Burundi. Sister Hall is active in ladies ministries and also teaches in the Bible school.

Chapter 3

Stuck!

by **Pamela Smoak**, Tanzania

The rains were not to start in central Tanzania for two more weeks, but the deluge pounding the roof of our Sheaves for Christ Toyota was proof once again that the unexpected always happens in Africa. We had carefully calculated this eight-day trip to end well ahead of the rains: two days to drive the 235 miles out to Western, four days camping in our tent beside the church teaching and preaching, and two days back. We did not make it.

Everything had gone as planned until a flat tire earlier in the day, the last of the eight. Then, the rain. It started as a drizzle. As it increased, we seriously thought of unpacking our tents, cookers, and food and just waiting it out. But this was unfamiliar territory with no towns and few villages—no hotels for one hundred miles. We were not sure how friendly the wild animals in area were either, so we kept going.

The roadbed was dirt with occasional boulders strewn in the middle. Five months of dry season had churned the dirt into a fine, powdery dust that was four inches deep and, in low places, six to eight inches deep. Brother Smoak had stopped even before the rains began to lock the hubs on our double-cab pickup so we would have the advantage of four-wheel drive as we forged our way through a dusty fog. The rain turned the top three inches of dirt into slick, slimy mud with several inches of the fine dust still beneath the surface. Driving was difficult.

We had left the town of Singida around two o'clock in the afternoon after having the flat tire repaired. At that time we had been confident that we would reach our home in Moshi by nine o'clock. At nine o'clock we were not driving through our gate but through a mountainous pass, still 150 miles from home. The truck had slid, pitched, and bucked its way for four hours in the rain when two immovable objects stopped it. Two large trucks traveling in opposite directions had met while each one was coming down a hill. As they met at the bottom of their respective hills, they slid in the mud, side-swiped, and became hopelessly locked together. Their slick tires and the slick mud prevented both of them from backing up to disengage their trucks. Several men from a large cross-country bus behind us and Brother Smoak and Pastor Massawe got out and tried to separate the trucks that were blocking the road.

Brother Smoak also examined the terrain on either side of the road with a flashlight. There was no way around.

When we returned to the truck, we examined our options. There was no way to go forward. A mountain cliff loomed our left, a dropoff plunged into a valley on our right, and a huge cross-country bus bottled us up from behind. Even if we could have turned around, we were on the only road through this part of Tanzania. To take a detour would involve back-tracking the six hours to Singida, going east to the coast, and then north to Mount Kilimanjaro and Moshi. That would be a two-day detour in good weather! We decided to sit and wait till the morning.

The rain on the truck roof made it difficult to talk and be understood, but just then we heard the voice of our five-year-old son, Gordon, say, "Well, I am going to pray that God will stop the rain and let us go home." That is just what he did. Then he curled up in his blanket in a corner of the

Stuck!

floorboard and went to sleep. Brother Smoak, Brother and Sister Massawe, and I got as comfortable as we could and fell asleep from the exhaustion of the day.

Just before midnight, we were startled awake by the sound of a diesel motor roaring past us, going up the hill in the opposite direction. The rain had stopped, the wind had begun blowing hard, and the roadbed had dried up enough so that the two trucks had disengaged. The road in front of us was clear.

Seven hours and 150 miles later, we rolled through our gate. We were home. Gordon awakened for the first time since his prayer the previous night to see that we were home. His only comment was, "See, I knew God could do it!"

• •

Richard and Pamela Smoak, former Associates In Missions in Kenya and alumni of Jackson College of Ministries, received their appointment as United Pentecostal Church missionaries to Tanzania in October 1988. Brother Smoak was the assistant pastor of the United Pentecostal Church of Bossier City, Louisiana, at the time of their appointment.

In Tanzania, Brother Smoak coordinates the Bible school and regional ministerial training programs and travels extensively to strengthen the churches and to assist in church planting. He also supervised the work of the national church while the field superintendent, Brother David Ward, was on furlough.

Chapter 4

Deliverance from Death in Rwanda

The story of Pastor Christia Mwenemwenye Kanyamwa
as told to **Darline Kantola Royer**, Uganda

The jingle of the telephone in our hotel room in Jinja, Uganda, startled us. Who would be calling? We had arrived in Uganda just two weeks earlier, and few people knew our whereabouts. When Brother Royer answered the phone, I heard him say, "Who is calling? . . . Oh, Christia. How good to hear from you. . . . Yes, you may come today. We do want to see you."

Many times since the outbreak of the genocide in the country of Rwanda, Brother Royer and I have prayed for Christia. We knew that he was pastoring in Kigali, Rwanda's capital, where the terrible atrocities and killings began in April 1994. Many months later we rejoiced to hear that he was still alive, but we had no news about his circumstances.

My first acquaintance with Christia began in 1984, when he was sixteen years old and the youngest student at Life Tabernacle Bible School in Nairobi, Kenya, where I was a missionary teacher. He had come to Bible school from Rwanda, although he was born in Zaire. Eight years had passed since he completed his three years of Bible training, but vivid memories of Christia marched through my mind.

As a student, he was quick-witted, energetic, studious, sincere, and full of youthful zest and sometimes frivolity. He could speak French, Swahili, and more than seven tribal languages, but not English. Within one year he learned English well enough to translate from Swahili into English. The accordion fascinated him, and soon his daily practice enabled him to begin playing for chapel and church services. He put his heart and soul into preaching the Word of God.

As the memories marched by I recalled his graduation day and reflected on the mental and spiritual growth that marked his years in Bible school. How thrilling it was, eight years later, to see him walk onto our hotel veranda, extend his hand in warm greetings, and say, "I am so happy to see you!"

As we sat overlooking the headwaters of the Nile River as it flows north out of Lake Victoria, Christia shared his story and answered our many questions about his life and ministry since he returned to Rwanda in December 1987. His deliverance from death in the midst of the genocide in Rwanda testifies of the protecting hand of God upon His servant. I share his story just as he told it to us in March 1996.

When I [Christia] returned to Kigali, Rwanda, in 1987 after graduating from Life Tabernacle Bible School, I assisted my pastor for one year. In 1989 I opened a new church in another part of the city and continued pastoring there until July 1993, when I was called back to pastor the mother church. When the president of Rwanda was killed in April 1994, war broke out and killings began after two days. I felt much concern for my saints. Both Hutus and Tutsis were in my church. At that time we had a group of eighty people. After the war began, we were not able to have any more services. I have heard that our building was bombed and destroyed. When trouble started, I began moving around the city to check on the saints.

To move around, people carried a panga [a large knife] or a stick. I refused to carry either, because as a man of God, I did not want to be thought of as an enemy. I met my first opposition after the second day when I went out from my rental house to see about the saints. As I was walking without a panga, a soldier arrested me. He asked, "Why no panga or stick?"

I replied, "I am a pastor, a man of God!"

The soldier said, "No man of God, no pastor; everyone is equal." He tried to force me to take a panga. But I insisted that I could not, because I was a man of God. When I refused, he called me an enemy and said, "Choose death or life. Get a panga to live or be killed!"

Some of the soldiers in the group knew me as a pastor. They argued among themselves about me because I refused to take the panga. The chief soldier pushed the others aside and raised his gun. Others began to shout, "You can't kill him like that. He is a pastor." Then they pushed me and told me to go. So I went back home.

When I reached home, I was told that a saint had been killed. I went to see about the report. Arriving there, I found both the man and his wife on the ground dead. The children were missing. As I was returning home, I felt sorrow and was crying. On the way I met soldiers who asked me, "Why are you crying?"

I said to them, "Some of my saints were killed. That's why I am crying."

This annoyed the soldiers, who said, "How can you call our enemies, the Tutsis, your saints?" The soldiers then called me the enemy because I was pastoring Tutsis.

A soldier then said, "If you are a true pastor, your God will save you." They made me stand in front of them and asked for my identity card. I showed it to them, and they said, "Let us go together and kill people."

I replied, "For me, no; I can't! When I walk with you, I'll also be involved in the problem."

The soldier said, "We'll kill you now!"

At that time another group of soldiers came. One of them was my saint. When he came he removed his cap, saluted me with, "Pastor!" and asked, "Pastor, what is going on here?"

I told him, "They are trying to kill me."

This soldier and his friends then took me and escorted me home. When I entered my house, I was thinking about the saints. So I closed my door, which was not allowed. While I was there crying, other soldiers came. They found my door closed and began pounding on it. I opened the door, and a soldier asked, "What are you doing in you house with the door closed?"

"As a man of God, I am praying," I answered.

"You are praying when others are in problems. If you are praying, you must have peace," the soldier said.

"My Bible tells me when I am in a problem, I also need to pray."

Then they asked, "Why did God allow our president to be killed like that, for he was a good man? You must be involved with our enemy."

I tried to say, "No, I am not your enemy!"

Then they told me to come out of my house. I went out. They got a neighbor. They handed me a panga and said, "Now if you are on our side, just kill this man and then you can go. It is simple. Just kill and nobody will hurt you."

My answer was, "As a man of God, one who preaches the gospel, I am not allowed to do that."

They asked, "Who doesn't allow you to do that?"

"It is my Master who doesn't allow me to do that."

"Who is that Master?"

"It is my God, Jesus Christ!"

The soldier then said, "We are your god now. We have your life in our hands."

I replied, "No, you can't be my God. I have a Master, Jesus Christ, who is God. He is the only One!"

They responded, "If you want to argue, then you must die!"

Some of my friends tried to plead, but they refused. Others tried to persuade me to just kill the man and go. But I continued to tell them I could not kill. I told them that in my country, Zaire, we do not have the practice of killing.

Then the soldiers pushed everyone aside and made me stand alone. They said, "We will count to three. When we reach three, if you do not kill the man, you will die."

I saw myself as dead and prayed aloud, "God, if this is Your way, just receive my heart."

The soldiers asked, "To whom are you praying?"

"To God," I said.

"To God?"

"Yes, because it is only God who can save me from your hands."

They shouted, "If you are sure it's God who can save, let Him do it now. Kill the man or you will die!"

"No!" I declared.

They began counting. "One!" People tried to insist that I just kill the man and go. The soldier's gun was pointed at me. I heard "two" and then "three."

Just as I heard "three," some men jumped toward the gunman and pushed him. Two bullets passed just above my head.

They called to me, "Pastor, why are you waiting now? Just leave this place and go." I had on a suit and new pair of shoes. I pulled off my shoes, dropped them, and began running. As I ran down the road, bullets passed overhead. The enemy forces were shooting at one another from opposite sides of the road. I fell on my knees and crawled along the road.

After some time I arrived at the home of one of my saints. I found the father, the grandmother, the brother of my assistant pastor, and six children. Sensing trouble, the adults crawled under the bed to hide, and I pushed the children into the house to join them. I returned outside to get the sev-

enteen-year-old son. As I was trying to persuade him, a grenade landed between us. Both of us fell backwards, and I lay shocked for maybe five minutes. Just as I raised up, another grenade came. I forced myself to run into the house. After ten minutes, someone came from outside and told us, "The boy is dead."

At that time I recognized it was only God who had saved my life. Then we went out of the house and brought the body inside. I stayed for three days in this home and helped them bury the boy. During this time I learned that many saints had fled to Zaire or had gone to the embassy.

After three days I decided to go to the embassy of Zaire. When I left, I took the youngest boy, age eight, from the home with me. Later the Red Cross took this family to Zaire. On the way, I heard bullets passing overhead. It took me five hours to walk a distance that usually took forty-five minutes.

On the way I passed the home of my sister and found no one there. Then I heard crying. Inside the house I found my sister's two-year-old son, who had been left when the family had to flee. I carried the boy with me and continued on to the embassy.

For two weeks I stayed at the embassy with the two boys. We slept outside on the ground. We had no privacy and no bath. Food was a problem, and we had no shelter from the rain. I prayed for God to help us. Then a vehicle came, and I was offered a ride to Zaire.

The vehicle left us in Bakavu, where I found friends and was able to stay for a week. I attended a church, and the saints gave us money for transport to the camp in Goma, Zaire. We rode in a car to Lake Viva and crossed the lake on a ship. When we arrived in the camp, I began looking for my saints. In the city of Goma I found Pastor Jacque, a Hutu Rwandese who had been in Bible school with me in Nairobi. I rejoiced to find that he was alive.

After two days in the camp, where conditions were so bad, I remembered that my elder brother was in Kampala, Uganda. I decided to go to the border of Uganda and explain my problem in keeping two small boys. At the border they accepted me as a refugee and gave me a ride in a matatu [van-type taxi] to Kampala.

When I arrived in Kampala, I stayed for two day at the police station while looking for my brother. We slept on the floor and ate with the prisoners. I heard about a gospel crusade and went to the place. When they asked for testimonies, I stood up, gave my name, and testified. My brother's friend heard me and came to me. Then he took me to my brother's home. For over one year now, I have been staying with my brother and taking care of the two boys. I received news that the father of the older boy has disappeared and the mother is now staying in Zaire. Another child died, and she is trying to feed the three remaining. My sister is not able now to take the small boy. The boys now call me "Father."

No doubt Christia's story has been repeated over and over in various ways in thousands of Rwandese families. We rejoice with him in his deliverance from death. Our greatest joy is that Christia is an Apostolic preacher who has remained faithful to truth in the face of death. His greatest desire is to continue preaching the word of life. We believe that his faith and the prayers of many have kept him alive that he may preach the gospel of Jesus Christ. The prayers of God's people make a difference. Let us pray that God will call people of faith, such as Christia, to bring Apostolic revival to Uganda.

After thirty-three years of ministry in California and the death of his wife, Arlon Royer launched his personal involvement with foreign missions by ministering in seven countries of Europe. In 1990 he visited Kenya. There he courted and married Missionary Darline Kantola, who had received her appointment to Kenya in January 1986.

The Royers continued their ministry in Kenya until their 1993 appointment to Uganda, where they now serve as the first resident UPCI missionaries. They spent their first year following deputation in obtaining church registration, work permits, and a permanent place to live. By May 1996 they were able to hold the organizing conference for the United Apostolic Church of Uganda. At this conference fifty-four people received the Holy Ghost and twenty-nine were baptized in Jesus' name as nearly seven hundred Ugandans gathered to celebrate.

Chapter 5

The Story of Mala Baral of India

by **Stanley Scism**, South Asia

A young lady, Mala Baral, petite and poorly educated and recently converted from Hinduism, is making an impact in her Hindu community. Here is her story—a praise report and a prayer request.

Simon moved from the West Bengal Himalayan foothills to New Delhi, India, in search of a job. There he met a young man, John Samuel, our pastor's son, who witnessed to him and brought him to Jesus Christ. Simon invited his cousin, Narendra Baral, and another Hindu young man to visit him and to look for a job in Delhi, too. Narendra came to Delhi and to our church. He soon gave his heart to Jesus Christ and was baptized in Jesus'

33

name. He asked to attend Scism Christian Institute, and we admitted him for the following year.

When he arrived, he brought along his baby sister, Mala, eighteen, who also wanted to be a Christian but who knew almost nothing about it. She came to Bible college, was baptized in Jesus' name, and that year both of them received the Holy Spirit. Just before the end of the school year, their mother died, and the family blamed these two, saying that by becoming Christians they had angered the gods, who had then killed their mother.

Narendra had a family to support and a job offer in Nepal, so he left. Mala faced the family's opposition alone —with no church, no pastor, no fellow Christians.

She came back to Bible college the next year knowing that as the only Christian in her area, she would have to be strong—no one at home would comfort her. When she went home after her second year, the big idol was still in the front of their home and her father was still a drunkard, but she was much stronger in faith. She started a Sunday school for the neighborhood children. She let her light shine, and her witness radiated. Her sister was baptized in Jesus' name. After nine months of work, when the time came for Mala to return to Bible college, her family's idol and alcohol were both gone.

I paid her way to Gangtok, Sikkim, where she and another young lady from the Bible college led revival prayer meetings, bringing about the first real revival led by Indians that Gangtok has known. She came back home praying for her family to receive the Holy Spirit, too.

She conducted church every Sunday morning, Sunday school on Sunday afternoons, and house prayer meetings seven nights a week. On May 31, 1997, after the evening prayer meeting, she and her family went to bed. During the night she awakened to a noise. She went to her sister's bed, where she saw her sister speaking in tongues. When her sister finished praying, Mala asked what had happened. Her sister said, "I couldn't sleep, so I started to worship and praise God. Then I received the Holy Spirit in my bed and began speaking in tongues."

On June 9 Mala prayed for her sister's daughter to receive the Holy Spirit, and she did that evening. This is a dark area—these were the first two people to receive the Holy Spirit in the whole countryside.

Mala asks us to pray: "I want them to be strong in God. They just now came from Hinduism, so they might get in any kind of trouble. They have to be strong in faith in my absence, too. I have to go to Nepal for my job. I told you my problems. [She needs to make a living and does not want to be a burden to her parents, and an opening has come at her brother's school.] If I go there, I will put everything in God's hands. He will take care of His children. I know God's work is more important than any other work, and I want to do His work, but I have this problem. I am praying to God. I know He will surely solve my problems, and I request you, too, to please pray for this subject. This harvest here is plentiful, but the workers are few. I am asking the Lord of the harvest to send out workers into His harvest field. We three daughters of Christ are praying for you. Please pray for us, too."

Please pray also for more workers in the massive harvest field of India.

••

Stan Scism is the third generation of missionaries to bear the Scism name. Brother Stanley's grandfather, Ellis Scism, founded the United Pentecostal Church of India. His father, Harry Scism, is the general director of Foreign Missions Division of the United Pentecostal Church International. Stanley, born and reared in India, received his missionary appointment in 1987. He founded the Scism Christian Institute, named in honor of Ellis Scism, in New Dehli. Brother Stan Scism works and ministers in several nations of South Asia

Chapter 6

"The Unknown God" Found in a Heathen Temple

by **Tom Bracken**, Taiwan

It was a warm, sunny afternoon as we rounded the corner and stepped into the huge temple courtyard. Brother Graham, our visiting evangelist from Okinawa, Japan, and I had been walking around the area and observing the various craftsmen carving and painting idols, large and small. Now it was time to show him the third floor of the temple.

We had just finished a tremendous series of revival meetings in this city of Kaohsiung, and the Grahams were scheduled to leave the next day. I do not usually frequent the temples, as it is so sad to see the people thonging, bowing, and scraping in front of false, man-made gods. This, however, was a little tour with a purpose. There was something specific I wanted to show Brother Graham before he returned to Okinawa and his responsibilities in the U.S. Air Force.

The courtyard in front of the Taoist temple is expansive. It is there that many public events and spiritual demonstrations take place. As many as two to three thousand people gather there to see stage performances of Chinese operas and puppet plays—most having to do with the supernatural—play the mobile gambling machines, or watch striptease and other kinds of dancing.

Intertwined with the carnival atmosphere and the buying and selling are the powers of darkness "showing off" their prowess. This usually takes the form of demon-possessed Taoist priests or shamans going into trances and then telling fortunes, casting spells, pronouncing blessings, or bloodletting. Added to this are the fires. People feed the furnaces with fists full of special paper money called "hell banknotes." This "money," sold at the temple, is believed to enrich those who dwell in the place of departed spirits, or hell. The money with the thin patch of silver foil is for their ancestors. The ones with the gold are for their gods.

The devil seems to prefer doing much of his work in the night, so in the early afternoon we found the courtyard empty. We began to cross it and walk toward the steps that span the entire front of the temple. As we approached the series of some twenty or so steps leading up to the first level of the temple, I noticed a man sitting at the top staring at us. He looked to be around twenty-five years old and wore a loose shirt, pants, and sandals.

It is not unusual to be stared at here in Taiwan. We foreigners tend to stick out, and with Brother Graham being about six and a half feet tall, we really drew attention wherever we went. But there was something about this man's stare. It was so confrontational.

I began to stare back as we proceeded to climb the steps. Although I was not looking for a fight, I did not feel to take my eyes off his. He appeared to be demon possessed and hostile. Most likely he was a shaman, a spirit medium.

All questions of his feelings toward us were answered as we approached to approximately twenty feet of him. It was then that he spat toward us. I was not sure if his actions were due to a general dislike for foreigners or some spiritual enmity. I chose at that point to ignore him, and we walked on by.

We entered the temple through the huge, red doors painted with giant door gods, and we proceeded to the inside staircase on the left. Few people were in the temple at this time, as it was hot and humid and also during the afternoon rest period. Still I estimated that between fifty and a hundred people were milling around inside. They were all busy arranging food offerings on tables, bowing their heads to the ground, burning money in the inside furnaces, or just chanting prayers. They would stand in front of one of the three large idols that occupy the prominent positions of the first floor. Here the elderly, middle-aged, and young would touch the lighted incense sticks to their foreheads as they prayed and then turn and add their incense stick to the many others in the altar of incense.

We continued up the stairs as we glanced at the goings-on of the first floor. I explained to Brother Graham the important aspects of the layout of the temple, the placement of idols, and how they related to what I was about to show him on the third floor. We passed another furnace on the second floor and took a quick look into the main altar room of that floor. I pointed out that this floor had only one large, prominent god. Then we moved on.

Peering inside the third-floor altar room and seeing it was empty of worshipers, we began to enter. Suddenly, from a door on the opposite side of the room, entered our one-man welcoming committee. He had been climbing the staircase on the right side of the temple as we climbed the left. He approached us, still staring at me and trying to look intimidating. I ignored this and proceeded to explain what I knew about the altar before us.

This floor was different. Although there were literally hundreds of small idols on the walls and embedded in six-foot-tall cones, in the center, at the focus of attention, there was no idol. There was only a plaque with words engraved on it to the effect: "The God of heaven."

In the past when I inquired about this "God of heaven," I was told, "Oh, yes! We believe there is a god out there who is above all other gods. We just do not know what he looks like or what his name is." So, in this temple and in many other areas of their lives, they made a place for this "God of heaven" that they do not really know.

"You see," I told Brother Graham, "they can't make an image, because they do not know what he looks like. And they can't call upon his name, because they do not know his name."

While discussing with Brother Graham the similarities between this and what Paul the apostle experienced on Mars' Hill, I kept noticing the shaman out of the corner of my eye. He had moved to the center of the room, mounted a stool in front of the altar of incense, and lit an incense stick. He was directly in front of the altar; we were standing about ten feet behind and to the left.

He kept trying to get our attention, so finally I looked at him. It was then that this shaman did the first of several strange things. Placing his incense stick carefully into the ashes of the altar, he scooped up a set of divining blocks. These blocks are about four or five inches long, made of red-painted wood, and are in the shape of a crescent. They are flat on one side and rounded on the other. When cast to the floor, depending upon how they land, they give the inquirer an answer: yes, no, or try again (based on both flat sides down, both round sides down, or one of each).

Instead of casting them on the ground, knowing he had our attention now, he proceeded to stuff the blocks into his mouth! This caused his cheeks to bulge and his lips to stretch tight. The shiny red blocks showed through his parted lips. This sight, coupled with his wide-eyed expression, gave a comical, ridiculous appearance. Casually shaking my head, I said to him in Mandarin, "That was senseless." And then I looked away.

That was not the effect he desired. As I began to talk to Brother Graham, who now was half listening and half praying, our attention was once again drawn to this man. He removed the blocks and began to speak in words that Brother Graham could only guess at, but words I understood only too well. With an arrogant look he declared loudly, "The God of heaven is greater than Jesus!"

So here it was. That is what the animosity was all about. The demons in him did not like the Holy Ghost in us! There was no more avoiding the issue, no more ignoring it. It was time to confront. I quickly interpreted what he had said for Brother Graham, who began interceding. Then, answering his distorted declaration with the truth, I said, "Jesus is the God of heaven!"

His nostrils flared as he raised his hand containing the slippery divining blocks. He spoke loudly and with supposed authority, "I said, 'The God of heaven is greater than Jesus!'"and cast the blocks to the cement floor.

I looked down at them and said, "See!" for his blocks had landed in the "No" position. He clenched his teeth and bent to pick them up as I interpreted for Brother Graham.

Brother Graham, who was now praising God and speaking in tongues, continued to intercede. I had explained that in this method of inquiring in the temple, one must come up with the same answer three times in a row, or it does not count. So, on we went. As this shaman prepared to cast his blocks for the second time, he once again declared, "The God of heaven is greater than Jesus!" It sounded somewhat weaker this time.

As his hand came down I shook my head "No" and, sure enough, the blocks turned up another "No" answer. Again I told him, "See! Jesus is the God of heaven," adding, "and He loves you!" From this point on my contempt turned to compassion, and all I could feel was pity and a concern for the shaman's soul. I knew that Satan had bound his soul, had twisted his mind, and had him abusing his own body. I interpreted as he retrieved the blocks once again.

With a very subdued spirit and a low voice, we heard him say, "The God of heaven is greater than Jesus."

Sure enough, the third, confirming "No" was lying on the floor. I shouted, "See!" and Brother Graham shouted praises to God.

The defeated shaman gathered up the tools of his trade and said, "Okay, Jesus is as great as the God of heaven."

I responded, "No! I said, 'Jesus is the God of heaven!'"

He repeated my words and cast the blocks half-heartedly. "Yes" was the answer! I told Brother Graham. Was he having a good time in the Spirit!

Our shaman was not having such a good time and stood there, looking dejected. I felt it was time to zero in on his spiritual need. I began to tell him about this Jesus, whom we preach—about how Jesus wants to deliver him and save him. As I talked of the God who created him and how He does not like for us to hurt our bodies, the shaman began to back up. His countenance changed. His eyes went wide and his face contorted. I thought, Here we go again. But I knew that the power of Jesus' name was greater than anything this fellow could come up with and felt no fear.

He backed in a semicircle to a bench that lined the back wall of the altar room. From beneath it he pulled a bag. It looked like a small duffel bag and contained items of incantation—his bag of tricks. Crouching and trying to look very mysterious, he unzipped the bag and took hold of something. I think he wanted us to worry, but I kept telling him what the true God wanted to do in his life.

Then he pulled a doll from the bag—not an ordinary doll, but a fetish for casting spells. He did not know that none of these things could harm us. So, as he moved toward the middle of the room, I just stood there slowly shaking my head. He then began to move in the martial arts form of the *t'ai chi ch'uan* discipline. Holding the fetish high in one hand and moving in slow circular motion, he mumbled on. Just as he was really getting into it, standing on one foot and the other extended, an unintended thing happened. His doll's head fell off, dropping to the floor!

This, of course, was laughable, but I did not feel like laughing. I began to press, "You need Jesus. These gods aren't real. They can't help you. Jesus gave His life so that you can be saved." I had stopped interpreting for Brother

Graham. I trusted that he would understand what I was doing, and he did.

The man lowered his head in embarrassment, knelt down, and slowly picked up the head. Putting the head and doll back into his sack, he began to nod, saying, "Yes, I do need Jesus."

I thought we were finally getting through when, once again, he began to turn defiant with a foul look on his face. The demons did not want to let him go. He began to look quickly around the room. His eyes fell on a large ashtray that was full of cigarette butts. Hurrying to it, he dumped it into his hand and proceeded to stuff it all into his mouth. Some unclean spirit was causing him to stick things into his mouth. Strange. He stood there staring wide-eyed.

Shaking my head slowly, I responded, "That was senseless, really senseless."

Seeing we were not scared or impressed, he reached over and picked up a large bottle of black ink. This ink is used when shamans go into trances and with a brush write out a fortune or other communication from the spirit world. Taking the lid off and throwing his head back, he poured the whole bottle of ink into his mouth on top of the cigarette butts.

How pitiful this man was. Not wanting any more of this nonsense, we began to take authority over his tormenters. He went limp, with his head drooping and filth dripping from his mouth. His powers were of no effect. He was a defeated devil worshiper, yet he had a soul that Jesus died to save. We gathered around him. Brother Graham prayed and I ministered. He now seemed to be in his right mind. The three of us went to a sink just outside the door, where he dug the filth out of his mouth and rinsed it.

As Brother Graham and I prayed for this man, Mr. Lin, the wonderful presence of the true God of heaven, Jesus Christ, filled the place. He replaced torment with peace, and we knew this man's life would never be the same again. He seemed to understand and accept everything I was telling

43

him. I told him the tall one was leaving the next day, but that I would return to see him. He was so different. We left awed by what God had done.

I have returned to that temple several times but have yet to locate him. Please pray for him. There is hope, for now this man has felt His presence and knows His name!

••

Graduates of Conquerors Bible College in Portland, Oregon, Tommy and Sandra Bracken first felt God's call to Taiwan in 1979 and shortly thereafter began studying Mandarin Chinese at the University of California at Berkeley. They received their appointment as United Pentecostal Church missionaries to Taiwan in May 1980. Brother Bracken, a former U.S. Navy Seal, stated, "Our work is classified as pioneer missionary work. While opening this field to the whole gospel, we are involved with pastoring, training nationals (Bible school), translating and printing literature in Chinese, and opening new preaching points." Brother Bracken is the UPCI's official representative to the Republic of China and coordinates the Associates In Missions program and the World Network of Prayer in his field.

Chapter 7

How Do You Tell a Hungry Soul She Cannot Have a Bible?

by **Evangeline Rodenbush**, Europe/Middle East

It was an experience I will never forget! We were in Bulgaria. We handed out Bibles as fast as we could for hours without a break, and I never even felt tired. I only wished we had had more time and more Bibles to give.

How do you reach a former communist nation with the gospel now that those doors are open? Perhaps through the children? A children's crusade was planned. It was the burden and vision of Sister Thetus Tenney to plant the seed of God's Word into the fertile soil of the Bulgarian children's hearts. She had the ability, contacts with the Bulgarian government at that time, and strong faith in the Lord. Added to this was over one year of dedicated hard work to plan the meeting and raise the needed funds, including money for ten thousand Bibles in the Bulgarian language.

A Bible for every child who came to the crusade was the plan. It was advertised everywhere: "Every child who comes will receive a Bible." A large truck arrived with ten thousand Bibles ready for distribution. Everyone was excited. I was just happy to be there along with several other missionaries

How Do You Tell a Hungry Soul She Cannot Have a Bible?

from Europe/Middle East Region and other helpers who had come with Sister Tenney to be a part of this great endeavor.

The day finally came. Much to our surprise, an estimated twenty thousand people showed up. People were everywhere! My job was to help give Bibles to the children, so I found my place, along with several others, at the back of the truck.

We quickly discovered that we had a problem. As we started to give out the Bibles, people began to crowd in, reaching out as far as they could with their hands for a Bible. The police had to set up barriers around the back of the truck to control the crowd. Children were pushed and shoved toward the truck as those behind tried to get to the points of distribution. We actually helped to rescue some small children by pulling them through the barriers and sending them out under the back of the truck to keep them from being hurt.

The joy we felt at the response was exhilarating, but my heart soon began to ache as I realized that hundreds of old people had come and stood in line for hours, hoping to get a Bible. "Could I have a Bible, please?" they asked, reaching out with worn, calloused hands. "The Bibles are for the children. Please come back later," we told them. "For my grandson, please!" a woman begged.

What were we to do? The Bibles were to be given to the children first, and we had only ten thousand. This is the way it was advertised. It was agreed that the Bibles must be reserved only for the children.

But how do you tell a hungry soul that she cannot have a Bible? Sadly, I cannot describe the grief in my heart. I wanted to cry out, "This is not right! We have so many Bibles in America . . . in every room of the house and even in the car. Bibles are everywhere and we do not even really appreciate God's Word as we should. Why should we be so blessed while these people beg for a Bible, not having had one for so many years?" My heart ached as I saw their sadness, disappointment, and even tears as we told them again

How Do You Tell a Hungry Soul She Cannot Have a Bible?

and again, "I'm sorry, the Bibles are for the children. Maybe if you wait until the end, we will have some left."

Is it possible that the children may not have even understood what they were receiving? Bibles had been banned in Bulgaria and other communist countries for forty to seventy years. To the children, it was just a book; but the older people no doubt remembered when they had a Bible. Probably their Bibles had been taken from them, and for years they had only the Word that they had hidden in their hearts. To them this was no ordinary book. They knew what a Bible was, and they wanted one desperately.

One little old lady, after being told she could not have a Bible, went over, sat down on a bench, and cried. Sharon Turner took her picture. It is a picture that I will never get out of my memory. I cannot forget how helpless I felt. How do you meet the needs of the hungry when you only have a limited amount of food? I am happy to report that someone did slip a Bible to this lady. But there were many others who still do not have one. When we closed the back of the truck that day, many still stood with their hands out. I went to my room and wept.

I will never forget those faces. I will never forget how they kissed our hands when we gave them a Bible. I will never forget the look of those who did not get one. And I also remember the words of Jesus: "Inasmuch as ye have done it unto one of the least of these . . . ye have done it unto me" (Matthew 25:40).

••

Brother and Sister Robert K. Rodenbush have been involved in foreign missions ever since their appointment to Ghana in 1968. In their ten years in Ghana, Brother Rodenbush helped to open several other West African fields including Ivory Coast, Nigeria, Cameroon, Togo, and Benin. In 1979 the Rodenbushes returned to the United States, and he became the coordinator of Overseas Ministries. In this position he supervised foreign Bible schools, developed literature, served as principal of the annual School of Missions, initiated the Associates In Missions program, and coordinated Compassion Services International.

In September 1990 the General Board of the UPCI appointed Brother Rodenbush to replace the retiring Robert McFarland as the regional director for Europe/Middle East Region. As such he oversees the missionaries and national churches in an area spanning approximately 13,461,000 square miles and encompassing over 1.2 billion people.

Sister Rodenbush labors beside her husband and is a frequent speaker at ladies meetings.

Chapter 8

Stories of Eastern Europe

by **Cheryl Craft**, Eastern Europe

George Craft teaching at the Bible school in Izmail, Ukraine

In Izmail, Ukraine, a concerned mother asked Brother George Craft and Brother Samuel Balca to pray for her seventeen-year-old son, who was sick. When they arrived at his home, they discovered that he was paralyzed from the waist down. He had been injured in a motorcycle accident. The bones of his back protruded at the place of the break. The doctors had not done anything to help his situation.

Brother Balca and Brother Craft prayed for about forty-five minutes but saw no evidence of a healing taking place. When they prepared to leave, the young man began to shout, "I feel my big toe. I can move it!" Brother Craft, Brother Balca, and the family gathered back around the bed to see. The Lord inspired Brother Craft that this was like the

49

small cloud Elijah saw rise up out of the sea. The small movement of the toe would result in total healing just like the small cloud brought a torrent of rain.

Six months later, Brother Craft returned to Izmail for a Bible school opening. At the school dinner, he asked the pastor how the young man was doing. The pastor said, "He's here. You may ask him for yourself." He called the young man to come to their table. He stood and walked to them without any aid. He was completely healed and had resumed a normal life.

He said that healing had come little by little. Each day he regained feeling in his legs and feet. Before Brother Craft left that evening, the young man's mother asked him to pray again. "My boy's foot is just a little crooked. Please ask God to straighten it completely." She had learned the lesson that God can do anything and had the faith to ask Him to supply all her needs.

In a service in Hungary, a young Gypsy mother asked for prayer for her eight-year-old son, Winnie, who had leukemia. The boy was in the hospital. Brother Craft and a local pastor prayed over a handkerchief and told her to take it to her little boy and pray. She went to the hospital over the weekend and prayed as Brother Craft had instructed her.

On Monday morning when she visited the hospital, the doctor came running to her with a paper in his hand. He was speaking loudly. "A miracle! A miracle has happened in my hospital for the first time." He showed her the blood test analysis that had just been taken. The blood platelet count had been very low, but after the anointed handkerchief had been brought to the boy, the blood count returned to normal. The boy was released from the hospital and is in good health today.

Many small Gypsy churches are in northern Hungary. They have no church buildings, so they meet in their homes. As many as forty people will squeeze into a small living room to worship. One night in service, God moved in a special way and several Gypsies were filled with the Holy Ghost. A Gypsy pastor came up and very abruptly asked for prayer. He had heart trouble and high blood pressure. Then he announced very loudly, "I need more of that Holy Ghost." They prayed.

In a letter from Brother Craft's translator, we later learned that the pastor was healed, and the people were amazed at his zeal and his fervor for God. He had not displayed such fire for God in all of his life. The Lord supplied all his needs, physical as well as spiritual. This incident brings to mind James 4:2: "Ye have not, because ye ask not." Jesus said, "Ask, . . . [and] ye shall receive" (Matthew 21:22). For this Gypsy pastor, asking was receiving.

Brother Craft travels through three countries to reach the Ukraine: Hungary, Romania, and Moldova. The highways of Romania and Moldova are very dangerous. They must be driven on slowly because they are full of holes. The holes are so deep that it seems the car just falls into them. The highways are also dangerous because of road pirates. Authorities warn people not to drive at night.

One day Brother Craft was returning home from the Ukraine and had been delayed at the Moldovan border by security guards who accused him of being a spy. This delay made him late driving through the mountains of Romania. As he came over a hill, the sun was beginning to set. The reflection of the sun's ray caught on glass in the roadway. At the same moment, he noticed movement from the woods at the side of the road. It came from a truck with two men in it. They had hidden the truck in the woods. When they saw Brother Craft coming, they opened the doors to get out.

Their movement alerted him. All across the highway were big pieces of broken, jagged glass. It was a trap. In a matter of a few seconds, he realized their plan. He drove around onto the shoulder of the wrong side of the road and continued on.

As he drove away, he noticed the men in the rearview mirror. They looked at him and then stooped to rearrange the glass on the roadway. A gleam of light at just the right angle and at just the right time foiled their plans of robbery and hijacking.

The Scriptures say that God is a sun and shield for us. In this situation, the sun and shield protected a weary missionary returning home.

• •

In September 1971 Brother and Sister George Craft received their appointment as United Pentecostal Church missionaries to England and later transferred to the Netherlands. The Crafts faithfully labored in the Netherlands until 1991, starting works in Dordrecht and Hoofddorp. In 1991 the Foreign Missions Board granted the Crafts' request to transfer to Eastern Europe. They now use their home in Vienna, Austria, as a base for evangelistic outreach into the former Soviet Union and other nations of Eastern Europe. Brother Craft has been very involved in establishing and teaching in the Ukrainian Bible school.

Chapter 9

"I'll Praise Him"

by **Bev Burk**
Excerpted and condensed from *God Answers Prayer*
Copyright 1984, Word Aflame Press. Used by permission.

In 1976, a few months after our son Devon Paul was born, I was diagnosed as having granulomatus colitis. It seemed to cause no particular problem, so I saw no reason to change my lifestyle. My husband Dorsey and I still planned on going to Germany as missionaries, as we had since Bible college. In 1977 we received the long-awaited missionary appointment and made plans to live the rest of our lives in the country we loved so much.

I had discussed this change with my doctor. He said that since Germany was very modern, I should have no problem living there. Things were in order. I had done all I knew to do, and finally, after years of planning and hoping, dreaming and praying, we were on our way!

During deputational travel I started having severe abdominal pains—often severe enough to cause me to double over. This usually occurred two to three hours after eating and only seemed to be relieved by vomiting, thereby lessening the tightness in my stomach. I thought the extreme pressure a traveling missionary is under was taking its toll on my body and that things would certainly be fine when we got settled in Europe.

The day finally came to say good-bye to our friends in America and hello to our new homeland. It was love at first sight! Germany was much more wonderful than I ever thought possible. We soon found an apartment, bought furniture, started language school, and settled six-year-old Krystin in school. Life was wonderful—except for my health.

Many days I could not keep anything on my stomach. I had such severe cramps that I would wake my husband groaning in my sleep. I would lie in bed day after day on a heating pad trying somehow to stop the pain. I took strong pain pills, but nothing seemed to give any relief. When I was able to get up to do a few things, I would often have to hold to the wall or furniture. I lost weight until I only weighed ninety-seven pounds.

The German doctor finally put me in the University Hospital in Wiesbaden for very painful tests, which were repeated over and over. A psychologist came to find out why I would ask the doctors what they were going to do that day and why.

Finally, the wonderful day came when I went home. I was no better, nor had they told me anything about my disease. I was simply sent home without one word. However, I was more than happy to leave any way I could.

Up to this point I have not mentioned God. There is a basic reason for this rather obvious omission. I had not allowed Him to be involved. I was handling this. If the German doctors were correct, if all of this was caused by tension—if I was too intense about life—then all could be cured by relaxing. I really tried to do all that I was told. But I kept going, without asking God for His direct help. I was strong willed, and I felt that I could do whatever necessary if I really made up my mind to do it.

Soon after I came home from the hospital, a strange thing happened. For three nights in a row I dreamed that I was in an airplane, my spirit was very heavy, and somehow I realized that I was taking an emergency leave. Next to me

"I'll Praise Him"

sat a woman in a brown, flowered silk dress. I did not understand this at all.

In May 1979 my mother called from her hospital room in Portland, Oregon. She had just been told that she had cancer and had only six to nine months to live. We had no idea that she was even ill. For days I went around in shock. Should I go home? Should I wait? What could be done? All during this time I was still extremely weak.

Sometimes there is one incident in life that changes an entire story. Mine came one day when I had cried until I was too weak to cry any more. I was sitting in the living room—not thinking, not crying—just sitting. I had put some records on the stereo, trying to collect myself. One of Bill Gaither's songs suddenly caught my attention. The words were:

> I will praise Him,
> Knowing that my praise will cost me everything.
> I will praise Him,
> Praise Him with the joy that comes from
> Knowing that I have held back nothing
> And He is Lord.
> He is Lord.
> HE IS LORD!

Praise! To praise, not holding back anything at all? Praise, knowing it would cost everything I had? This sounded impossible, but sitting in Wiesbaden on that day in May, I knew that somehow I had to learn how.

I sat crying and praying. That day I told God I had no idea how to accomplish this task, but if He would guide me, I would do all I could to learn. I began by thanking Him that I had such terrible nerve problems, that I was a wreck and had made myself that way. Next I thanked Him for my mother's illness; that I had a sixteen-year-old sister that He would have to care for and help grow up; and that my father was going to have to try to pastor a church, teach full time in public school, raise Lurissa, and still try to stay sane.

Needless to say, it did not sound very thankful, but it was a start. I felt a burden lift, and I knew that was the answer I had been looking for.

The next day, I was once again unable to leave my bed, but it was with a different attitude. I thanked God—really thanked Him—and life was good. During that day, I thumbed through the Book of Psalms. I was impressed by the many times that David said, "I will." "I will praise the Lord" (Psalm 7:17). "I will praise thee" (Psalm 9:1). "I will be glad . . . I will sing praise" (Psalm 9:2). Throughout the Psalms, it was the same theme: I have problems, but I will praise.

Starting to learn to praise by praising for everything seemed a little too difficult. So I started by going one hour, stopping, kneeling, or if I was confined to bed that day, bowing my head and praising God for everything that had happened during the previous hour. Soon I could praise God for all that had happened during that time span. I could praise Him that I had to hold the wall and try to dust. I could praise Him that I could eat two and three bites of supper. I could praise Him that those two and three bites of supper had not stayed down.

Praise changed everything. I became happy, almost excited. Even when I was very sick, I still could learn to look for things to praise for. It became an all-consuming task.

One day I was extremely weak. Several people had told me how terrible I looked and I really needed to gain some weight. I knew that. But I also knew that I could not keep anything down long enough to get any nutritional value from it. I started reading the Bible to receive some encouragement from somewhere.

I opened to Psalm 41: "Blessed is he that considereth the poor: the Lord will deliver him in time of trouble. The Lord will preserve him, and keep him alive; and he shall be blessed upon the earth: and thou wilt not deliver him unto the will of his enemies. The Lord will strengthen him upon his bead of languishing. . . . An evil disease, say they, cleaveth fast unto him; and now that he lieth he shall rise up no more."

I could not believe what I was reading! It sounded like David had been with me the last few days! That chapter became the fort to which I would run whenever I felt discouraged, and I would find comfort there.

Romans 8:28 also changed me. I had read and memorized this verse as a child. I had read and memorized it as a teenager. I had read and memorized it as a young adult. But when I started to praise God for it, I learned how to use it. I thanked God that whatever this disease was and whatever it involved, it was for my good. I really started to appreciate the lessons I was learning from it.

Summer and fall came and went, and I continued to learn to praise. By constant practice, praise became a continual attitude. I could smile and really be joyful even when it hurt. I could be thankful even when I could not get out of bed. I could praise when I could not keep food down. The circumstances had not changed a bit. I still woke up my husband by groaning at night. The pain was terrible. But I had changed.

Christmas in German was so much fun! However, I could not get away from the feeling that I had better keep things up. One night I had the dream about the plane again and told my husband, "Let's get everything ready. I'm going to have to go to the States soon."

We checked airline schedules. A pastor in California had told us that if we needed anything to let him know. We called and he was wonderful. Yes, he had meant what he had offered, and he would be glad to help.

The first week of January, my father called from Portland. The doctors had operated on Mom and had given her just a few days to live. If I wanted to see her alive, I had better come home right away.

Thank God, He was in control. Everything was ready. I simply packed the suitcases and got on the plane. As I sat there, I looked at the lady on my left. She was wearing a brown, flowered silk dress. God never allows anything to come our way that He has not prepared us for!

On January 29, 1980, my mother passed on. Her last words were, "Oh, what a beautiful light!" Because I had learned to praise, her death did not devastate me.

After Mom's funeral, my aunt, my sister-in-law, and I tried to organize things for Dad and Lurissa. All this time I knew I was getting weaker. Towards the end of the job, my aunt and Miriam had to do most of it. I just could not seem to get it done.

Finally, things were as settled as the three of us could make them, and I felt it was time to go home to Europe. By now I could barely get through the day without going to bed, but I felt that if I could just get home and rest, I would be fine. I really missed my children and my husband, and I wanted to go home.

I was scheduled to leave at 8:00 Thursday morning. During Wednesday night's Bible study, I really felt sick and weak and spent most of the service in the restroom. On the way home, Dad talked me into going to the hospital for some pain pills to help me get back to Germany. After an X-ray, I was told I had an intestinal blockage and would have to be admitted.

It was hard to praise that night. I missed Dorsey and the children so much, but it felt good to get a shot and have some relief from the pain.

A day or two after admittance, a specialist came to tell me I had Crohn's disease—that there was no cure and it would plague me all of my life. An immediate operation was necessary to remove the blockage.

Soon after the operation, in which the doctor removed three feet of small intestine, I felt strong enough to wonder about this strange disease. I discovered that Crohn's disease creates small nodules or masses of inflamed tissue that penetrate into the wall of the intestinal tract. It often skips around in the bowel, so it cannot be cured by surgery.

One doctor later told me that when he tells someone he has Crohn's, he is sentencing a young person to a lifetime of pain and suffering from which there is no escape. He said, "I would rather tell someone they have cancer instead of Crohn's. At least with cancer they usually die."

Another doctor told me that if I had not had the surgery then within six months the buildup behind the blockage would have caused my intestines to rupture, after which I would have had about twenty-four hours to live. "Would the pain have been any worse?" I asked. "No" was the answer. Then I realized that had I gotten on the plane, I would have died. I spent a long time thanking God for His mercy.

My health improved, and three months after I left the hospital, I returned to Europe. I was feeling great and ready to do our part for revival in Europe.

My husband and I had a burden for the city of Munich, and we made plans for the move. My husband had gone to Munich with the moving truck, and the children and I followed later in our Sheaves for Christ car. I was enjoying the lack of a speed limit on the autobahn when construction narrowed the road. The car on my right jerked into my lane. Out of reflex action, I twisted the wheel away from it, putting my car in the oncoming lane. At speeds of eighty to eighty-five miles per hour, there seemed no way to avoid death, but at that moment I felt the warmth of Someone's hand over mine. The car immediately straightened—in the correct lane. At the next rest stop, Krystin, Devon, and I had ourselves a praise service.

Munich was wonderful! I enrolled in a new language school. We started to make contacts. I was feeling good. It looked as if the battle was won.

In the midst of the good time, I told God I wanted a meek and quiet spirit. (See I Peter 3:4.) Not long after my prayer, I became ill again. Eventually my health became so poor that Dorsey called Brother Scism for advice. A month to the day after we had dedicated our chapel in a glorious service—much like Solomon must have experienced at the dedication of the Temple—the Foreign Missions Administrative Committee decided that we should return to the United States on an emergency medical furlough.

We spent the night before leaving at the home of Brother and Sister John Goodwin. Everyone except me went on to service. I walked the floor wondering how I could ever make a sixteen-hour plane ride with two small children. At 9:00 I suddenly got relief. It was instantaneous. I did not ask why. I simply thanked God.

We flew into San Francisco and immediately went to the church in El Sobrante. An elderly sister walked up and asked what had happened to me on Wednesday at 2:00 AM. She said that she had been awakened with a tremendous burden and had spent those early hours interceding for me. Two o'clock in the morning Pacific Standard Time was 9:00 PM in Germany. God was still controlling things!

After the medical examination in Portland, Oregon, the doctor decided that I should be given a colostomy. This surgical procedure reroutes the intestine to end at an opening (an ostomy) in the abdominal wall and bypasses the rectum. I opposed the surgery with all I had. No way would I wear a bag to catch the waste.

In October 1981, I decided the quality of life I was enduring could not be worse than living with a colostomy. So in early November I had the surgery. Two weeks later I had another surgery to remove yet another intestinal blockage.

In December, Brother Harry Scism called my hospital room to talk to Dorsey. The workload at Foreign Missions Division had grown to the point that they needed someone to help, primarily in the area of publications—promotional items such as the *Global Witness* and training materials for use in the foreign Bible schools. Would Dorsey be interested? There was much rejoicing that day! God was giving us another area of foreign missions to serve in!

After our move back to St. Louis, my health became worse and then tolerable—only to revert to worse. Back and forth. In the hospital for tests. Out for a few weeks. Back in for more tests. In one year I was in the hospital seven times. I knew there was a blockage, but the tests did not show it.

In March 1983 my doctor came running into my hospital room. The blockage had been found. Surgery was quickly scheduled, and in the preoperative discussion, Dr. Berwald mentioned that he would probably take out the rectal stump.

The first thing I remember after surgery was seeing my husband beside my bed having a terrible time sitting still. As soon as he saw I was awake, he said, "They can't find any Crohn's!" "That's nice," I replied and went back to sleep. As soon as I really awoke, I immediately remembered what Dorsey had said. There was no visible Crohn's! The next day the doctor told me that a slipped staple from a previous operation had caused the blockage.

While thinking about the last seven years, I realized something often overlooked. God can speak a body in or out of existence. This is not a great thing for Him. But God cannot change an attitude or a spirit. He can provide the climate, but the willingness to change has to be generated from a submissive and contrite Christian.

One night I became discouraged because of some problems with my colostomy that developed since I decided to write this article. I asked God for a verse of Scripture, and Philippines 1:6 immediately came to mind: "Being confident of this very thing, he which hath begun a good work in you will perform it until the day of Jesus Christ."

On four separate occasions, one of the goals of surgery has been to remove the rectal stump. Each time, for a different reason, it was not done. After the last surgery, the doctor admitted he was not sure why it was not done. But I do. The colostomy will be reversed. God has promised and it will happen.

The disease of Crohn's has been a positive one. I have learned how to praise. I have learned more about faith. In fact, I have developed my own definition of faith: Faith is ability to relax in adverse circumstances, knowing they are for our good.

I do not know what the future holds, but with God's help, I will continue to raise my hands and sing, "I will praise Him. . . ."

••

The above article was written in 1984. Since then surgeries have whittled Sister Burk's intestinal tracts down to six feet of small bowel. Short bowel syndrome forced her to rely on intravenous feedings on a nightly basis for her nourishment for four year. Following numerous complications related to her condition and treatment that eventually led to endocarditis and open-heart surgery, she was told that her long-term survival depended on a small bowel transplant. She was placed on the transplant list at the University of Wisconsin Hospital in August 1995. In August 1996 a series of tests at Barnes Hospital in St. Louis, Missouri, indicated that she still needed the transplant.

Some thing happened, however, between August and November 1996. Sister Burk checked into Barnes Hospital in early November for a final test before the Barnes staff listed her as a transplant candidate. However, her physical change between August and November so astounded the doctors that they put off the experiment. Instead of performing the procedure, they simply monitored her for a week.

At the end of the week they concluded that her absorption rate had increased over twenty percent in two to three months. She could now maintain her weight and health with what she could ingest and with shots to supply additional magnesium. The doctors stated that a small bowel transplant was not needed at that time or in the foreseeable future. They could give no medical reason for the sudden change.

In December 1996, Sister Burk's permanent IV line was removed. For over a year she lived without the nightly feedings. However, in December 1997, following a bout with flu and other minor illnesses, a new IV line was inserted and the nightly intravenous feeding began again temporarily.

The miracle that Sister Burk anticipates has not yet occurred. However, a greater miracle continues as she praises God daily. She learned a very important lesson as a missionary in Wiesbaden, West Germany. Because of that, her life has changed.

Sister Burk is now a substitute elementary teacher for a suburban St. Louis public school district and volunteers at the World Network of Prayer. Her husband is an executive assistant for Foreign Missions Division.

Chapter 10

The St. Petersburg Revival

by **William Turner**, Russia/Kazakhstan

Not since the days of the late Andrew Urshan has St. Petersburg, Russia, seen such a Oneness Pentecostal revival. As I write, Sister Turner and I have just returned to Moscow from a joyous weekend in St. Petersburg, where a very young Apostolic church is continuing to flourish in spite of strong opposition. Nearly ever quarter of the Christian community has spoken against them in a city where just a few years ago the communist government was the principle persecutor.

The religious community there is being stirred by a bold proclamation of the oneness of God and the Acts 2:38 salvation message. In one year's time, Pastor Igor Tsibh and his wife, Nina, have seen their group grow from thirty to crowds of over six hundred on Sunday nights in their rented hall just off of the city's main street, Nevsky Prospect.

The Jesus Name revival first came to St. Petersburg over eighty years ago and spread across Russia, south to the lower Volga River, east to the Ural Mountains, and beyond. In spite of years of arrests and persecution under Soviet communism, the Oneness message gained a foothold in the Baltic Republics and Belarus to the west and the Ukraine to the south. There are still groups of Oneness believers in these areas whose grandparents told them stories of Andrew Urshan.

After years of persecution, however, many of these older Oneness groups have settled into traditions of guarded worship that inhibit a Holy Ghost revival. The biblical principle in evidence in 1916 nevertheless applies today: "Blessed are they which do hunger and thirst after righteousness: for they shall be filled" (Matthew 5:6).

God is bringing revelation to a new generation in Russia that hungers for truth. Some traditional Oneness leaders who have opposed freedom of worship and the ministry of the Spirit are being bypassed by this latter-day outpouring. The soil of the Russian soul is ripe for a revival of truth for those who dare to sow and those with a will to reap an end-time harvest.

In 1916, on the eve of the communist revolution, thirty-two-year-old Andrew Urshan, newly arrived in the czarist capital after preaching a Holy Ghost revival among the Baptists in Tbilisi, Georgia, was invited to preach to a group of St. Petersburg evangelicals. The meetings were held on Soljanoy Lane, in a building still in use today.

During a two-month period, about 150 people received the Holy Ghost, and approximately that same number were baptized in the name of Jesus Christ in St. Petersburg's Black River. The rumblings of revolution forced Andrew Urshan to return to America, but a fledgling Apostolic church continued.

Igor Tsibh and others like him are not direct descendants of that early revival. They came to a scriptural revelation of the mighty God in Christ by another route. When communism fell in Russia in 1991, Igor was a successful oral surgeon. As he adapted to Western medical technology, his lucrative practice expanded. So did a burgeoning drug addiction. Before long, his newly acquired wealth was gone, his life in shambles.

The St. Petersburg Revival

He attended a charismatic church in St. Petersburg and experienced a dramatic conversion and powerful filling of the Holy Ghost. He was instantly delivered from drugs. He attended a Bible school and became a pastor in a small city on the shores of the Baltic Sea. Eventually he became a leader of a newly established trinitarian organization in the St. Petersburg area.

Brother Igor's understanding and love for the truth of the oneness of God and the authority of the name of Jesus Christ began through a question asked by a man in his church. It was very similar to the incident that led to Andrew Urshan's acknowledgment of the truth of baptism in Jesus' name during his time in St. Petersburg eighty-one years earlier. In each case, a man in the congregation came to the preacher, pointing to a verse in the Book of Acts that clearly stated that the church of the apostles baptized in Jesus' name. In both cases, those young men, separated by three generations, embraced truth.

In time, Brother Igor's understanding grew. It was an obvious progression from the truth of baptism in Jesus' name to an understanding that the God of the Old Testament was the same God who came in flesh to establish the New Testament.

Just over a year ago Brother Igor resigned his position in his former trinitarian organization and moved his congregation to the heart of St. Petersburg. An opportunity came to preach on the local Christian radio station. During a question-and-answer program, he explained his belief in the oneness of God and baptism in Jesus' name. Word began to spread of this "new teaching," and soon Bible study crowds began to overflow. Attendance on Sundays skyrocketed. A Holy Ghost, Jesus Name revival began, accompanied by healings and miracles.

Last winter, nearly every denominational pastor in St. Petersburg joined with the Orthodox Church in signing a letter condemning Pastor Igor's teaching. He was no longer welcome to speak on the Christian radio station. Instead he was regularly denounced over the air. Sunday attendance dropped from of high of six hundred to half that number, but those remained faithful.

In the past few months, Sister Turner and I have grown close to Brother Igor, his wife, Nina, and their eleven-year-old son, Vladimir. We were introduced to them through one of our workers in St. Petersburg. Along with six other small churches in the area that look to him for leadership, Brother Igor has indicated his desire to work in fellowship with the United Pentecostal Church International.

In the past year he has baptized over 250 people in Jesus' name. Nearly that many have received the Holy Ghost with the evidence of speaking in other tongues.

During our recent visit, we rejoiced as over forty people were baptized in Jesus' name on a Sunday morning. Most of those had already received the Holy Ghost. About ten had not. In a prayer meeting after the baptisms, six more people received the Holy Ghost.

One sister had been attending the church for some time but had resisted baptism in Jesus' name. She had told Brother Igor, "I was baptized in the titles Father, Son, and Holy Ghost, and I have enough faith to believe that is equal to baptism in Jesus' name." She changed her mind, declaring, "I don't have faith to believe that anymore. I want to be baptized in Jesus' name."

I had the pleasure of preaching in the service that night. How appreciative those precious people were to hear again that they have brothers and sisters of like precious faith around the world. How wonderful to see them rejoice in the same truths that thrilled my heart when I came to God over twenty-five years ago!

Two more people received the Holy Ghost that night, including a grandmother who had been nearly deaf. When the Lord filled her with His Spirit, He completely restored her hearing. I heard her shouting and embracing people, saying, "I can hear! I can hear!"

The revival continues. After the previous visit, we made the train trip of over five hundred miles back to St. Petersburg to teach on the subject of holiness at Brother Igor's request. He conducted two months of intensive study for his congregation on the subjects of holiness, the new birth, and the oneness of God. As our textbooks, we are using Brother David Bernard's books on these subject, which we have had translated into Russian.

It is time for truth to be proclaimed in Russia once again. And God is raising up people who will lift their voice to declare it.

••

Brother and Sister William Turner, home missionaries in Astoria, Oregon, received their appointment as United Pentecostal Church missionaries to Korea in October 1978. Thirteen years later, the Turners became the first UPCI missionaries to Russia and Kazakhstan. Brother Turner is the official representative to these nations, pastors a church in Moscow, and is president of the Southern Ural Bible Institute in Orenburg, Russia. In August 1995 Brother Turner also became area coordinator for the Commonwealth of Independent States, specifically including Armenia, Azerbaijan, Georgia, Kazakhstan, Kyrgyzstan, Russia, Tajikistan, Turkmenistan, and Uzbekistan.

Chapter 11

The Kang Family Story

by **Helen White**, Indonesia (Retired)

To my knowledge the Kang family consisted of the father, the mother, one son, and two daughters. The father was from mainland China, and his wife was a Java-born Indonesian. Many of those who came from China were affluent, but not this family.

The older daughter was married and did not attend church. Ing, the younger daughter, was in her late teens and attended church regularly but was not a radiant Christian, as she had not received the Holy Ghost. Bing, the son, attended a Protestant church. Mama Kang loved God but was a weak, sickly woman and was not able to attend church regularly. Papa Kang was a very faithful brother and was always the first to arrive for the daily 5:00 AM prayer meeting.

Finally Ing became hungry for God and joined in the afternoon prayer service. As she yielded herself to God, He filled her with the Holy Ghost and she spoke in beautiful English as the Spirit gave utterance. She really had a good experience. Brother White wanted to baptize her, but she refused. She wanted her brother there for her baptism.

Sunday morning Bing came but sat at the rear of the auditorium. Several young people tried to welcome him, but he did not warm up to them. When Ing went up to the platform to the baptistery, I noticed she motioned for him to follow, but he did not budge. As Brother While started to put Ing down into the water, she began to speak in English by the Holy Ghost. Bing just sat there and acted as if it was nothing unusual. Some of the young men tried to persuade him to go up close, but to no avail. Someone said, "Don't you hear Ing speaking English?"

"That is that Sister White," he answered sarcastically. But Ing continued speaking in English, quoting Scripture and saying, "And this is the same Jesus!" Several of the young people persuaded Bing to come closer. Before long tears glistened in his eyes, and he began earnestly seeking the Lord. Soon he too was speaking in tongues by the Holy Ghost.

Papa Kang enjoyed his salvation. He was unable to converse much in English, but he was always attentive to the preaching of the Word. Many times he had a "glory spell" during the preaching, and the folks rejoiced with him.

One morning we were called to pray for Mama Kang. The family said she had a fainting spell and fell in the street. When we rushed into the house, she was lying on the bed, looking lifeless. We could find no vital signs. We prayed, prayed, and prayed. Finally she began to stir. Papa insisted we pray and pray again and again. God came on the scene and gave her a definite touch. She out-lived Papa Kang.

Bing attended Bible school and began pastoring a small congregation after finishing the course. He married a young lady who had been in my first Sunday school. She was a consecrated girl and faithful. In later years they moved to Surabaya, and now they both pastor churches. They have ten children, several of whom live in America. Both Bing and Meta have visited me at different times.

I thank God for fruit that remains.

The Kang Family Story

In 1938 George and Helen White left Missouri and founded what became known as the United Pentecostal Church of Indonesia on the island of Java in the Dutch East Indies. They served in Indonesia until ill health and age forced their retirement in 1974. Brother White went to be with the Lord in 1976. Since then Sister White has returned to Indonesia six times to teach in the Bible school and minister as a short-term missionary. Age has not diminished her burden for missions.

Chapter 12

Of Fleas and Miracles

by **Judy Addington**, New Zealand

My husband often hold revivals, seminars, and other special services for many Maori pastors. Some are unable to pay him but show their gratitude by taking him hunting or fishing on Maori land.

After the close of a particular meeting the pastor took Brother Addington to his small house. Brother Addington was to sleep on the couch, but the room where the pastor and his wife slept was adjacent to the living room and was without a door. Not wishing to cause uncomfortable feelings, Brother Addington asked if the pastor had a sleeping bag, for he wanted "to go out and sleep under the stars." Willing to oblige, the pastor proceeded to the barn, where three dogs were lying on an old sleeping bag. After arousing them and shaking the bag, he gave it to Brother Addington.

Brother Addington went out onto the surrounding pasture with a flashlight to guide his way. Finally finding a spot on a hill, he proceeded to bed down. After a short while he could feel strange proceedings occurring inside the bag. Taking the flashlight he peeked inside. Lo and behold, a

New York City of fleas was marching to and fro. It was too cold and too late to return to the farmhouse, so he zipped up the bag and let them feast.

Later that night a hog came up and tried to eat an orange that Brother Addington had brought with him. And then, to top it off, it rained!

My husband came home with over two hundred fleabites and memories that will bring us laughter for a long time to come.

Since our arrival in New Zealand in 1986, our church has always met in homes, school halls, or rental buildings—cost preventing us from purchasing a building. This has been a great deterrent to our effectiveness. Some people just do not attribute stability or repute to churches that do not exhibit status or permanence. We have prayed and looked and sought after a building, but the doors were consistently closed. We did not have enough money! But God's timing is not ours, and He can go through any door—even one with no handle!

In November 1997 God miraculously opened the door for us to purchase a building through the witness of one of our church members to his boss. And it was not just any building either! When God does things, He really knows how to bless abundantly. This building is only three years old. It has a huge upper floor, newly redecorated, that was a former club with adequate kitchen and toilet facilities. Below are two businesses that hold leases, and with their payment the church can afford the balance due monthly.

The millionaire owner—with whom we have found favor—is willing to hold the mortgage at a lower interest rate than we could get through the bank and has been very accommodating. The building is zoned both residential and commercial, giving us a broad access. This building is also more than adequate to open our Bible school training center, a daycare, and even a Christian school in the future.

••

Robert and Judy Addington received their appointment as United Pentecostal Church missionaries to New Zealand in 1984. They located in Christchurch on the South Island and have labored primarily among the European majority.

Brother Addington states, "In 1995 we divided our main church in Christchurch into four separate groups—three European and one Maori—for greater outreach in the city. Our Maori church became very involved in radio ministry each week, and it has proven to bless churches in both the South and North Islands. The UPC of New Zealand, under the leadership of Ringa Hei Hei, welcomes a greater effort to reach the European and Asian peoples. We thank God we can all work in harmony for a New Zealand revival."

Chapter 13

Halu Village Glorifies God

by **Esther Henry,** Papua New Guinea

The place we went for our crusade was a little village called Halu (pronounced ah-loo). As we neared the Western Highlands-Chimbu border, we pulled off the highway onto a dirt road and continued for about one-half hour. We had no idea where the place was. However, we would see some of our church members walking to the conference, and they would give us directions. We were told to park the car inside the gate of the political member's house up the road.

We parked the car under the stilt house and got out. We

Missionary Brian Henry and the Mudmen of Papua New Guinea

thought we would be sleeping in the house and that the crusade would be close by. We were in for a big surprise when our guide informed us that we had to walk to the village where we would sleep and hold services.

A couple of Bible school students helped with our luggage and we set off. It was quite nice for the first few minutes of walking through coffee groves and gardens. Then the path turned to the right and we discovered that we had been walking the crest of a small mountain. From the curve, we looked straight ahead to the crest of another mountain, where ant-size figures were waving at us.

Our guide, one of our UPC pastors, said, "Just beyond those people you see is the village where we will stay."

We gulped and thought, Here we go! as we began our descent into the valley. After walking down, down, down, we came to a deep ravine with nothing but a huge tree trunk bridging the gap and a river at the bottom. Brother Henry asked, "Um . . . do we have to cross that?"

The guide said there was another path going down to the river, through it, and up the steep bank on the other side. We chose that option.

When we reached the other bank, my sandals were all wet from wading through the river, and my feet kept slipping around as we ascended the side of the other mountain. At the river, our guide's wife met us, and from that point on she looked out for us the entire weekend. Once we crossed the river, our guide mentioned that we had just crossed the border into the Western Province.

We reached the village of Halu about an hour or so from the time we left the car. People began to weep and run to meet us, hugging us tight. It seemed the whole village was there to meet us. We found out later that we were the first white people ever to visit their village. One of the village elders told us the next day, "We have three little churches in this village, but you are the only missionaries to care enough to come."

Over the weekend the entire village showed up for the services. Many people repented and gave their lives to the Lord. Six people received the Holy Ghost, three were baptized in Jesus' name, and three were healed of various sicknesses!

The day we left, the same village elder told us, "People here in my village keep telling me that they are happy for the churches, but they feel no Spirit and want more. This weekend we have seen the Spirit of God at work, and I believe most of my people will go to your church."

On Saturday afternoon, we held a beautiful, cleansing, and rewarding footwashing service for the ministers. They had never practiced communion and footwashing in their churches and did not know what to do. After Brother Henry taught them for about forty-five minutes on this biblical subject, we began to wash one another's feet. As we began to do so, each one started to weep and pray for the other person. Not only did we wash their feet with water, they were also washed with tears! The tears came naturally. And when we were done, a spirit of intercession fell on all of us gathered in that little church hut.

One of the sisters came to me and through her tears said, "Oh, Sister Henry, I feel like I've been baptized all over again! I feel so clean!" I could not help but hug her and smile because I knew exactly how she felt: clean from head to toe, inside and out! The presence of the Lord was so powerful and His blessings were so rich upon us that day.

Over and over again the preachers testified, "We have learned so much! Now we know what our churches need."

The next weekend, the overseer and presbyter of that region held another crusade in that village. They installed a new pastor for the believers that were won as a result of this crusade. We are trusting God for the conversion of the whole village. That possibility is already within our grasp.

Since that time, the other churches closed down and pulled out of the village, and one of our former Bible school students is now pastoring the only church in Halu. Praise God for truth and victory.

• •

Brian and Esther Henry are alumni of Christian Life College. After his Bible college graduation Brother Henry became the administrator and secretary-treasurer for the United Pentecostal Church of Tacoma, Washington, and served there until he and his wife left for Papua New Guinea in 1994. After serving as Associates In Missions in Papua New Guinea for almost two years, they received their missionary appointment in January 1996. They are currently the only resident UPCI missionaries in Papua New Guinea. They live in Goroka in the Highlands and administer the Bible school. Brother Henry states that they have "a big job on our hands in training ministers and building a new Bible school facility."

Chapter 14

Saved by Superstition

by **Cecil Sullivan**, Philippines

Shane Sullivan with a hundred-year-old Kelinga woman.

It was March 1990. My fifteen-year-old son, Shane, and I had been invited to travel to a remote, mountainous area in Northern Luzon, Philippines. We were anxious to visit another missionary's work, which was with the tribal people called the Kelingas. We were very excited, because we had wanted to visit some primitive tribes ever since our family had arrived in the Philippines as missionaries one year earlier.

It was early morning when Shane and I left

to catch a 7:00 Legaspi City bus to go to Tuguergarao, which was over 1,200 kilometers [720 miles] away. After two breakdowns on the indescribably bad road, we arrived in Manila fourteen hours later. Because of the breakdowns, we missed our connecting bus to Tuguergarao, forcing us to spend the night with our good friend and fellow missionary, Ken Fuller. We caught the next "7:00 AM bus," which, incidentally, left at 8:30 AM. It too had mechanical problems that had to be repaired before it could leave the bus station. Anyway, after a dusty, jolting, exhausting day, we finally arrived at Tuguergarao at 5:30 PM.

We had reservations at the Del Finn Hotel. However, on arriving we found that the hotel was closed to guests because a large gun battle had taken place inside the hotel before our arrival. In the fight, a Philippine general named Oscar Florendo was killed. He was a highly respected and beloved officer of the Philippine people. They allowed us to view the damage done by the gunfight.

The next morning a party of four, along with Shane and me, caught the jeepney at 6:30 AM to start our trip to Tabuk. At Tabuk we took another jeepney going up the mountain. This was a dirt road, very rough and dry. The jeep was bursting at the seams, and as is Philippine custom, many people were hanging along the outside.

Four soldiers were on the jeepney with us. This had its good and bad points. Sometimes the New People's Army (NPA) will open fire on a jeepney carrying soldiers, killing everyone in the way. On the other hand, sometimes the soldiers' presence will keep the rebels from robbing the jeep. You never know which way it is going to be.

One of the soldiers was a sergeant. He began questioning the three Filipinos who were traveling with us as to who we were and why we were going to Lubo. When he found out that we were missionaries, he did not like it at all. He told us we were "not welcome" and that we should "go back." He then proudly told us that he was Catholic and every time a Protestant came, it caused division and problems. Our two

Saved by Superstition

Filipino pastors talked with him for a long time, and we finally won his friendship. After that, he said no more about us going back.

About halfway along the journey, we were stopped by a military roadblock. The soldiers made everyone get out of the jeep. Seeing us, they said that they were going to search our baggage. This can take some time, and it also gives them a chance to steal personal items from the luggage. I got out my camera and, with a smile, told them I wanted to take all their pictures. (Thank You, Lord, for that inspiration!) The Filipinos love to have their picture taken. This venture caused them to put the luggage down and gather together for the picture. Then we all climbed back aboard the jeep, waved good-bye, and smiled to the soldiers.

The weather had been very dry, and the engineers were bulldozing a new road up the mountain. This we were very thankful for, because it saved us three hours' walking. We finally came to a halt at the end of the road. Yes, the road ended. At about 2:00 PM, the hottest time of day, we began our walk over the mountain by trail. It was a hard, five-hour walk, made worse by having to carry our backpacks.

About two-thirds of the way up, I stepped off in a small hole and twisted my knee. The knee started giving me quite a bit of pain, so I found a "walking stick" to ease the pressure. As I hobbled along, young a Kelinga woman, carrying a baby on her back, fifty pounds of rice on her head, and a bundle under her arm, passed us up. Upon seeing that I was having problems with my knee, she offered to carry my backpack. I thanked her for her offer but said I could manage. No way would my Irish pride allow me to go into the village with this lady carrying my pack along with all her other paraphernalia and me carrying nothing.

At around 7:00 PM we arrived very tired, very hungry, and very dirty. The village had no electricity, no running water, and a horrible smell, which we later found to be a mixture of pig and human manure. We were welcomed by a very gracious Brother Gamoud, a brother in the Lord, who took us to his home, where they prepared us supper of plain rice and a thin soup made of ant larvae and some vegetables.

After supper they showed us to our room, which contained a hard, wooden bed with a blanket on it. We tried to sleep, but it was impossible. About 2:00 AM we heard squealing and scurrying on the roof and discovered the sound belonged to a large pack of rats that came down the bedroom wall and scurried all around the bed. I quickly turned on my flashlight, grabbed a shoe, and started banging on the floor. This drove them into the other missionary's room. We heard him jump up and start banging on his floor. That drove them back to our side. Needless to say, we slept very little that night. This was repeated every night we were there.

The first morning when we got up, we asked where the restroom was. They pointed around in all directions and said, "Anywhere okay." We had to go to the river to try to find a private place to bathe—nearly an impossible task. More could be said about this situation, but I will not elaborate.

The population of Lubo village is about three thousand people. It has one Catholic church, but no priest. Upon inquiring I was told that someone had killed the priest with a bolo [large work knife] a few years ago during a tribal war. Lubo also has a United Pentecostal Church, thanks to Missionary Glenn Clark and his work among the tribal people.

That night we had a great service, held under Brother Gamoud's house as the houses are all built about eight feet off the ground. A large crowd watched from outside. I spoke on having faith in God. Many came to the altar and prayed, and God blessed us. The next night someone else preached, and we were blessed again.

The next morning, Thursday, we woke up hearing an argument outside our house. We knew trouble was brewing. Brother Clark shared with us a dream he had during the night. He said a man was chasing him with a gun and trying to kill him, and every time the man would start to shoot, Brother Clark would wake up. The last time the man broke

Saved by Superstition

through the door and was about to shoot when he awoke again. He told us he was troubled by the dream.

Thursday's night service had a large crowd both outside and inside. The service was especially blessed, and Pastor Corpuz was to preach. Shane and I were sitting on a bench in front of the congregation. One gas lantern hung from a nail above the altar. After singing we heard a loud scream somewhere out in the darkness from behind the church. All the people outside started yelling something, and then they all ran away. We knew we had better start praying and praying hard!

At first, I thought the rebels were attacking the village. Then I saw two men moving in the shadows. One had an M-16 and the other had an M-14, both machine guns. Both men had ammunition clips covering the front of their vests. I began to pray that God would protect Shane and that He would somehow let me get Shane out of the line of fire in case there happened to be shooting. At this time Brother Clark stood and asked the congregation to just go on worshiping and praying. He told Pastor Corpuz to go ahead and preach. Brother Corpuz did a terrific job under the circumstances. When he finished, we had an altar call as usual, and many people came praying. Some were also praying at their seats.

About this time it began to rain, but we did not learn that this rain was an answer to our prayers until the next day.

Shane was in the back of the church, praying with some men. I told one of the brothers, "Please, if shooting starts, take Shane and try to get to the jungle with him!" About that time, six rounds were fired from the M-14! I could tell that the rounds had gone over us—thank God—and not directly at us. We thought a rebel attack had started, but there were no more shots, just blessed silence.

A few minutes later one of the brothers in the church recognized one of the gunmen as his uncle and started calling out to him. They exchanged some heated words as the brother was trying to find out just why his uncle had "come to shot at me." While this was going on, the saints made a line, single-file, all the way from the church entrance, up the stairs, and to the door going up into Brother Gamoud's house. Then we were directed to go immediately up the stairs because these men meant to kill us. One by one we made our way up the stairs.

After a while the elders of the village came and sat in the tiny, lantern-lit living room with us, either on the floor or on the two-by-fours on the floor that served as a "sofa." They came as protection to us, knowing that the men would not fire on us with them present. We were comforted with their being there. Even thought we could not speak their language and they did not speak much of ours, I knew they were the Lord's doing.

The next morning's light brought some comfort. I climbed to the top of a hill and praised God, thanking Him for His divine protection. That day suspicious little groups of men met all around the village. Most of them were heavily armed.

Brother Gamoud, in whose house we were staying, immediately gathered the elders of the village for a conference. The elders rule Kelinga villages. According to Kelinga law, if a visitor eats with an elder's family, then he is considered under the protection of the whole tribe. This is like the salt covenant in the Old Testament. If someone violates that covenant, the clan law demands three lives of the family who violated it. I suppose leading an attack to kill visiting missionaries is a violation, even though no one was killed. So according to Kelinga law, three of the gunmen's family had to die.

Brother Gamoud bravely took the elders directly to house of the leader of the attackers, and the man then began begging for the elders only to kill him and not any of his children. Brother Gamoud then told him that according to the law of the village they must die, but because the Lord Jesus Christ had changed his life, he was going to forgive him for what he had done. He kindly explained that no blood would be required. This not only amazed the attacker but the whole village as well when the villagers found out what this elder, Brother Gamoud, had said.

That day many people began inviting us to eat meals with them. We had four lunches and almost that many suppers. I said, "I don't think I can eat another meal"—especially ant soup and pork entrails. But the brethren explained, "You must eat, for this is the people's way of showing the men who attacked us that the village is accepting you." This would make them afraid to harass us further or harm us.

That night I preached on being born again. The crowd was small, but eight people received the gift of the Holy Ghost! At the end of our service some outsiders still threw stones and hit the roof, but no further gunfire occurred. Neither did we conduct service as long as usual that night.

The next day the principal of the school invited us to her house to talk. She felt she could explain some things, for we had many unanswered questions. We explained that we still loved the people who attacked us and wanted no retaliation against them. She was astonished. After talking to her, we had the story put together as to what had happened. This is what we learned from her.

It seems that hearing people cry from time to time in the services disturbed the man who lived next door to the church. According to their customs, Kelingas do not cry unless a loved one has died. She further explained that the attackers could not see anyone dead. (But there were some deaths! Romans 6:2 says, "How shall we that are dead to sin, live any longer therein?")

The man then got together with four of his friends, and they began drinking while discussing the big problem of the "crying church people." As they drank, they began to discuss more fervently how to stop that church and make it go away. At first they were going to kidnap one of the members and threaten to kill him if the church did not stop. Then they decided to just kill everybody—then "no more problema." The next thing to settle was who would fire the first shot since the village law demanded retaliation. After more tuba wine, one man got really brave and said that he would be the one.

That night as they were coming towards the little church, a woman who saw their intentions began screaming a warning in the Kelinga language, "They are coming to kill you!" Normally, under different circumstances, you cannot run onlookers away, but that time they scattered like quail!

The men took their positions—two on each side and the leader at the back of the church. He was to fire the first shot, and then the rest would open fire on us all. But as we were praying, it miraculously started to drizzle. The two on the right side of the church moved out of position because they were getting wet. When the other two on the opposite side saw them move out of position, they did not want to be the only ones to fire into the service. So they held their fire when the leader fired over our heads, hoping that one of the others on the other side would kill the first one and they would be clear of the retaliation law.

Filipinos do not like to get their heads wet in the rain. They are very superstitious, especially in the mountains. Many believe that if they get their head wet, they will go crazy or become very ill. Normally we do not thank God for superstitions, but we did this time.

Through it all, God confounded them and worked a great miracle! Our lives were saved, and this opened the door for many more miracles and favor in the village. That Sunday three more people were filled with the Holy Ghost. Then Sunday afternoon, five were baptized in Jesus' name.

As we left the baptismal service, an elderly lady sent for us to come to her house. When we arrived we could see that her legs were very swollen and she could not walk. She said she had not been able to go out and feed her pigs in days. She had heard about the services and believed that if we would pray for her, she would be healed. We prayed for her in Jesus' name, and she got up and walked slowly back and forth. The next day as we were preparing to leave we noticed a great stir at her house. She was out feeding her pigs. The neighbors were all around her asking about her healing, and she was witnessing to them all about her miracle.

The next morning we began our long trip home. While riding on the bus to Manila, Shane said, "Dad, I have never been so scared in all my life."

I said, "Son, we were all afraid."

Then he said, "But I would love to go back sometime to see how they are doing!"

Now that is a missionary's heart.

••

Burdened for missions for many years, Cecil and Carolyn Sullivan received their appointment to the Philippines in 1987. Brother Sullivan first came into contact with the Filipino people while in the U.S. Navy in the 1960s. Two years after receiving the Holy Ghost in 1969, the Sullivans began pastoring the Fountain of Life Tabernacle in Zeigler, Illinois. They pastored there for seventeen years and also founded the Zeigler Christian Academy.

The Sullivans spent their first term in the Philippines teaching and establishing twenty new churches in the remote Bicol region. As president and teachers at Apostolic Center for Theological Studies (ACTS) in Manila, they ministered to and taught eighty students to be "revolutionaries for Jesus" during their second term.

Chapter 15

Our Great Welcome to the Kingdom of Tonga

by **Bennie Blunt**, Tonga/Western Samoa

On our very first night in our new home in Tonga—Tuesday, December 13, 1994—Sister Blunt was standing in the kitchen, drying dishes, when all of a sudden she had a feeling that something was not right. She glanced out the window. Much to her surprise, a man was looking in the window at her. She was so scared she could not speak or move her feet. She seemed glued to the floor. Finally, after what seemed like an eternity, she walked into the dining room, white as a ghost, and told me what had happened.

When I looked outside, the man was gone. Therefore, I convinced her that it was a banana tree leaf moving. After much persuasion, she accepted my theory.

The next three nights went by without incident. But Saturday night arrived. Sister Blunt was asleep and I was reading in bed about 11:00 PM. A small noise alerted me. Thinking something was wrong, I got up and looked out the sliding glass door of our second-floor bedroom. As the flashlight beam reached the end of the veranda, a big Tongan man stood up, slid down the pole to the ground, and ran away. We called the police, but they told us, "If you want to make a report, you'll have to come to the police station," which was three miles down the road.

After this incident, I felt I needed some kind of protection. However, since our container had not arrived from the Fiji Islands, the only thing we had in the house that was of any use was a cast-iron skillet.

On December 19 at 11:15 PM, we were sleeping very soundly when a loud noise awakened us. I thought someone was breaking into our house, and I was going to stop him or her! I jumped out of bed, grabbed my trusty cast-iron skillet, and ran through the living room and dining room and into the kitchen, only to find that they were already in the house. They had entered through a small bathroom window in the basement.

They were trying to leave but failed to undo the safety chain lock on the kitchen door. When I ran into the kitchen, I did my best rendition of a Cherokee war hoop! Earlier that evening, however, Sister Blunt had spilled water on the floor and had not wiped it up. I hit the water. My feet went out from under me. My left leg struck the bottom of the cabinet, and the impact gashed my leg. As I fell, my head hit the countertop, leaving a gash in my right eyebrow. Did I ever see stars!

The two intruders leaped over me and ran down the stairs. I heard one of them run across the basement and run into what was going to be my office. He jumped through a set of louvered windows. Well, there I was—half-dazed and angry. I went stomping downstairs—blood streaming across the stairs and down the steps—to find the second intruder. When I turned on the light, he was trying to hide in the corner. He started towards me. I told him, "Don't come any closer!" I guess that after seeing this bleeding sight and the mean-looking skillet, he decided to leave too! He cursed at me, then turned, held up his arms in front of his face, and jumped through another set of louvered windows.

We later heard through the "coconut telegraph"—the rumor mill—that they said they would be back since I had run them off. Christmas came and went. By this time our container had arrived from Fiji and our house was no longer empty.

On January 5, 1995, a stormy, windy night, the wind died down about 3:00 AM. Something awoke me. I felt that there was someone in our house. This time I approached the matter much more carefully, even getting dressed this time.

I opened our bedroom window and walked through the living room. I could see that the back door of the house was standing open. Evidently someone was watching the outside and alerted the man inside. He came running out of the office in a dead run. At this time I smacked the wall and hollered, "Get out of here!" They stole my impact drill and my circular saw and would have carried off much more if I had not awakened. The police came and took fingerprints, but nothing was ever recovered.

Needless to say, after about five months of living with a wife who jumped at every noise, we moved into the capital city of Nuku'alofa to a home in a safer area. Thankfully we have had no more incidents.

After visiting in the South Pacific, Brother and Sister Bennie Blunt sensed a new direction of the Spirit concerning their future. With much prayer, the leading of the Lord, and their October 1989 appointment as UPCI missionaries, Brother Blunt resigned the church he had founded in Wentzville, Missouri. The Blunts arrived in Fiji in September 1992, where they taught in the Bible school while he also pastored the Bible school church. In December 1994 Brother and Sister Blunt transferred to Tonga. Brother Blunt is the field superintendent of the Tongan church. They have established and teach in the United Pentecostal Bible College in Tonga. Brother Blunt is also the area coordinator for American Samoa, Western Samoa, and the Cook Islands.

Chapter 16

"Only You, Lord!"

by **Bennie DeMerchant**, Brazil

While the Cessna 206 floatplane cruised above the Amazon River fifteen miles west of Manacapuru in the early morning of February 20, 1993, the engine suddenly quit. Moderate rain beat on the windshield. I had been flying on instruments above a solid overcast with the occasional open area on the right, through which I could see the main river. In lowering weather conditions, my rule of thumb for IFR [Instrument Flight Rules] flying is "I Follow River."

This new engine had been installed the day before on Murumuru Lake, between Anori and Coadajas. The old engine had thrown a connecting rod on the previous flight, and an emergency landing had safely been executed. The plane had been waiting in the bush for sixty-three days for this new engine. This was its maiden voyage, and all systems had checked out perfectly before taking off. My mechanic, Francisco, sat in the co-pilot's seat by my side.

I was at about twelve hundred feet altitude when the engine stopped. No big deal. Fuel tanks run dry in flight. In a couple of seconds, with hardly any loss of speed or altitude, the engine resurges when fuel hits its injectors from the other tank. But the tank I had switched from still indicated it was almost half full of fuel. Automatically I switched to the opposite wing tank and pressed the auxiliary fuel pump switch.

The propeller wound down in the wind as the engine lost RPMs. It gave a quick surge and died again. It was unbelievable, but it would not restart. I could see the Amazon to the right within gliding range when the engine quit, but I had already lost three hundred feet of precious altitude. Waves on the water indicated a wind change—now from the south—that was quite strong. That would be the direction to glide towards the nearest open water, the river.

At first, the river seemed within gliding range, but after a while I had second thoughts. The strong wind was right over the nose. The plane—laden with parts, tool boxes, leftover mineral water, food, and bedding—sank rapidly as it glided down in the heavier, dropping, rainy air. It seemed incredible. I squirmed and looked in wonder with a big lump in my throat. At three hundred feet altitude above the trees, I could not glide to the river with such a rate of descent.

How quickly the calmness of the ride had changed. My heart raced as I sat upright, craning my neck for any other alternate place to sit down. The decision must be made now! Near the river's edge, beyond the trees, was a small cow pasture. This plane is not a chicken that loves land! It is a duck! Look for water! What are the other alternatives for a dead engine landing?

A glance confirmed that there were only small ponds in the jungle below, and they were too small to even circle. In this changing wind situation, the tension of judgment about the capabilities of the aircraft whose controls I had sat behind for thousands of hours brought my senses to their keenest point. However, I lacked the safest ingredient—altitude! There was much water, but it was beyond reach. In a normal, hot tropical day, rising air from convection currents and no head wind would permit an easy glide to the river with altitude left over on arrival. Now, in the rain and downdrafts, the glide rate seemed not much better than for a grand piano!

Mammoth samauama trees reached for the sky above their lower forest friends. They were the first to meet the level of our wing tips as we silently coasted down. I well knew how large these trees were since my walk around the base of one near our church in Paratari took fifty-two paces. They are enormous. There is enough lumber in one limb to build a wooden house. Some samauama trees stand over 125 feet high. I remembered one as a landmark growing up from low vegetation on an island that on a clear day could be seen on the horizon over twenty-five miles away.

From the side window I saw the tops of these trees go by level with the wings. I then realized how low we were, gliding with the airplane's only engine dead and visibility obscured by the rain. I craned my neck to see where we were going and prayed.

On long flights high above the jungle floor, I had often studied the possibility of making an emergency landing in the jungle. With no water reachable, I could go for the smaller trees in flooded, bushy creeks in the low areas between the hills. In the final phase, I would slowly stall the plane onto the upper third of the trees and hang on for the initial crash, which would be the hardest. If an engine-out landing procedure had been done in the jungle in this manner, the rest would be the rumble and tumble till the aluminum bird would come to its silent rest. I would then hold a "Thank You, Lord" service for being unhurt; grab a fishing rod, a few flies, a compass, and matches; and head home.

I did not count on a situation like this with rain beating on the windshield and forward visibility much reduced. I would do my best but would have to leave more than I wished with the guardian angel that I almost gave a heart attack on a few occasions.

I prayed repeatedly and earnestly, "Only You, Jesus! Only You!" Still flying, as I glanced out the side window I could look up and see the tops of huge trees at least fifty above the wing tips. Thoughts flashed! "Am I flying blind between these trees in this rain? What's next?"

I expected to feel and hear the pounding of ripping metal at any second. I held the plane in a slight sideslip for better forward visibility from the side as the plane's nose rose higher and air speed dropped further. The final glimpse from the slowly gliding aircraft revealed the impossible. I spotted the end of a short cow pasture, and we were right on top of it!

As the flaps extended fully, wet bushes shook as they brushed between the Cessna's pontoons. With its nose high, the plane made a rough squash and rumbled like a double wagon going too fast over a rough sidewalk. Pontoons dug into the wet grass and mud. At any second I expected to crash into a tree stump or hidden log in the grass, left by Amazon hand farmers to burn or rot out in time. I held the stick all the way back while the plane grabbed the ground, lurched forward, and tried to nose over in the beginning of a somersault. Miraculously, it just came to a sudden stop! It was still upright!

"Wow!" I exclaimed to the shaking Francisco, whose hand was under mine on the fuel selector switch. I have made rougher landings on big waves! This one, however, was in a field on wet grass with no wheels. I had seen pictures of some planes that had nosed over landing on lawns in *Seaplane Pilots* magazine. We were loaded almost to gross weight, landed "dead stick" in a small cow pasture, and had not upset! The plane had scooted to a stop on wet

"Only You, Lord!"

grass. The rain beat on the windshield and steamed up the inside as final prayers of gratitude filled our hearts.

I could not wait for the rain to stop and was curious to know what was torn up on this rugged flying flivver. I opened the door and jumped out on the left float. It seemed so high from the ground. Francisco slid across the pilot's seat and was behind me.

It was excitingly true. In the rain we searched in vain to find a bent, broken, or cracked float strut, fitting, or straining rod. I was overjoyed! All was intact. It did not matter if rain was soaking my shirt. The bottom of the pontoons and sides were normal. There were no dents anywhere. The floatplane just sat there proudly with its pontoon keels on the wet grass as if some angel with a hydraulic lift had picked it up in the warehouse and set in down right there!

Two keel marks in the mud and grass behind the plane indicated where it had first contacted the ground and came to such a quick stop. It had not even bounced!

I traced these marks in the rain to their starting point. I stared at the tall trees between which I had just flown. I studied how steep the approach angle had to have been. The only exact spot where the pontoons could safely touch in that incline was at that end of the field. How small was that jungle cow pasture! God, I thought, You have got to be great and the PeeKay floats on this machine mighty tough!

From the other side of a nearby house on the left, dogs started to bark. Someone opened the back window of the house and looked out in the rain. A big bird with two huge, white bananas under it had silently arrived from the sky and sat down in their back yard. Two soaked men joyously were gathered around it and acted so happy that they seemed crazy. A small child in its mother's arms looked through the window of the house as fear gripped her, and she started to cry. Just a short stone throw beyond the floatplane, down a steep riverbank, flowed the mighty Amazon, which the mighty bird had tried to reach in vain. Had the plane sat on

99

the grass field much beyond the point where it did, it would have helplessly crashed into the river as it went over the bank.

Pacing the pontoons' skid marks back on the grass, I found that the initial touchdown was made in a small mud puddle about fifty to sixty feet wide and about a foot deep in its center. Two rows of grass in the puddle lay parted from its midpoint towards me. I noted the freshly riled water in the center of this puddle, and being wet already, I waded out just to check its depth.

I now witnessed the point where the plane's pontoons struck first with a splash in the middle of that puddle on the initial contact of the landing, or I should say arrival, and from which it scooted to a stop on the grass. I looked all around. It was the only little puddle in that entire sloping field. This puddle provided a slippery ski action on impact that started the plane sliding upright in a relatively stable position as it skidded to a stop, high and dry.

Had the initial contact been hard on the land, the plane with such a cabin load could have easily nosed over, causing extensive damage or injury. I was totally overwhelmed and jubilant! "Only You, Lord! Only You! I could not have put that plane in the middle of the puddle again under these conditions if You had allowed me a hundred tries."

It had rained most of the previous night where we had dozed off in the hammocks inside the lean-to where we had finalized the aircraft engine installation. Everything had been checked out the previous afternoon and was ready to go. Why did the engine stop in flight?

Our search was short. I checked the fuel system drains of the plane. Pure water ran out, filling up the sampler cup and running over into my hand for some time. Finally the green aviation fuel appeared, and my hand felt cool as it started to evaporate. We had checked all of the fuel system drains before taking off the lake an hour ago. How could such a simple, basic, crazy thing as water get inside the fuel system and put us on the ground? New or old, there is no

"Only You, Lord!"

aircraft engine in all the world that will burn Amazonian water! It is not the engine's fault if rainwater gets into the system.

The plane had been waiting sixty-three days in the lake in the middle of the rainy season where it poured rain almost every day before the new engine was installed. Dew and mildew seemed to penetrate everything. I had ordered a new set of fuel cap filler kits that were back-ordered and never arrived. Under certain conditions and over time, the old type of fuel caps would allow rainwater to collect in the top of their seating wells on top of the wings. In time the sun hardens these flexible rubber O rings, and water collecting on the top from rain corrodes their fitting counterpart, which can allowed water seepage into the fuel tanks. In the floating hanger, the problem did not appear soon. With the plane out in the weather for so many days in the rainy season, the problem was revealed.

The wing tanks are flat bladders of rubber or vinyl material. They are rolled up, squeezed through a small hole in the top of the wings, unrolled, and laid out flat in their compartment inside the wings. Snaps hold them in place after drain and vent hoses are connected. If any foreign matter gets into a tank's vent pump or its automatic valve, the suction of the fuel pump can pull the bladder out of its external snap holders, leaving a large wrinkle in its flat bottom. When not discovered and refueled, these wrinkles in the bottom of the bladder-type tank can hold a pocket of water from faulty outer tank cover fillers that would be undetectable by system drain checks. The aircraft's movement and time would bring this undetectable water from there to the engine's injectors through the fuel system and stop the engine in flight.

That happened on this occasion, and the results were serious. Had it happened while flying above the lower fog bank that morning, the landing could have been worse.

After the rain stopped, we unloaded the plane, and a neighbor lowered a part of his fence. About fifty onlookers gathered, and for three hours many of them helped to cut and carry saplings to lay in front of the plane. They watched, pushed, or lifted till we finally got our unharmed Cessna back into the water. On checking the flotation, no new leaks were discovered. Immediately a new set of fuel filters kits replaced the old system lest our beautiful bird again be turned into an expensive golf cart.

••

Bennie DeMerchant felt the pull towards missions at an early age and started flying lessons in high school. After graduating from Apostolic Bible Institute, he and his wife, Theresa, ministered briefly in the Atlantic District before receiving their missionary appointment to the Amazon basin of Brazil in 1964. In 1970 Sheaves for Christ helped Brother DeMerchant acquire a Cessna floatplane, which took the UPC of Brazil into the huge rain forest area equivalent to half of the U.S.A. The area now has 160 churches, divided into seven districts. Brother DeMerchant has acquired 12,000 hours of single-engine floatplane flying and is the field superintendent of Brazil.

Chapter 17

In Deep Water

by **Theresa DeMerchant**, Brazil

"Mom, it hurts so bad!" Bennie Jo cried as they wheeled him in from surgery. He had just had a biopsy surgery on the bone in his upper right arm. The doctor consoled me that he was coming out of the anesthesia and would be all right. I had waited, prayed, and fasted all day and half the night, but I felt so helpless. I had to leave Jo in the care of the St. John Hospital and go back to my room at my brother-in-law's home.

It all happened so quickly in January 1991. Bennie Jo complained of a pain in his upper arm. He was fourteen years old and loved to do a lot of exercises. I told him to stop the pushups as maybe that would help his arm. He was stout and tall, broad shouldered like my brothers. His blond hair and honey-colored eyes made him stand out among his little, dark Brazilian friends. Even his school friends were all slender, and he tried so hard to be like them.

His dad insisted that I take him to a Brazilian clinic. After the X-rays the doctor called me in alone. He said it looked like bone cancer and if I had any way to take him back to Canada to do so immediately. We called the Foreign Missions Division, and the executives agreed. For some time I had felt impressed to pack my suitcase, for I would be going home very quickly. I did not know why. Now I had only four hours to get our tickets and pack for two. I did not believe the local doctors and thought we would soon be back in Brazil.

My husband stayed in Brazil as he had a national conference scheduled soon. Bennie Jo was so happy to be traveling to Canada that he skipped around the house and just gathered up some schoolbooks and games.

We landed in St. John, New Brunswick, in a snowstorm. Brother Ed Goddard's church was good to us. We waited three weeks for the results of the biopsy: Ewing's sarcoma. It was malignant. The oncologist said Jo had an eighty percent chance of survival. I received permission from the oncologist to go to the hospital library for more information. The books said less than fifty percent chance of survival. I did not tell Jo that. He called the floor doctor "Mr. Bad News" as I asked him to explain to Jo the reality. Jo exclaimed, "Just think, me, me with cancer!" I called Brother DeMerchant at the Brazilian national conference and said, "Ben, we are in deep water!"

We went through the routine of chemotherapy and radiation on his arm from January until June. Then we heard that Brother Anthony Mangun and Brother Billy Cole would be at Pea Cove Camp in Maine, not too far from St. John, New Brunswick. Jo wanted to go to that camp. We were staying at Aunt Geneva Kierstead's home in Perth-Andover. I packed for us to go the camp for the weekend and then to return to the hospital on Monday for the next chemotherapy treatment.

In the first service Bennie Jo went right to the front for the healing of his arm. We just knew God could do anything. Sure enough, Jo claimed his healing. His limp arm was strong, and he could swing it in every direction. I could not deny his exuberant testimony. "I'm healed, Mom! I am not going back to the hospital." I could not convince Jo to keep our appointment at the hospital, so we drove the 250 miles back to Perth-Andover.

On Tuesday the oncologist called me to come to the hospital. I explained that Jo refused the chemotherapy because he felt fine. She insisted we had to drive back the 250 miles to the hospital. The oncologist explained that Jo was only fourteen years old, thus a minor, and we would have to sign for him. I explained that my husband would be returning from Brazil at the end of July. She wanted to see us both as soon as he arrived. The chemotherapy was waived until the end of the month.

On the marked day, my husband, Jo, and I met the oncologist. She insisted that it was against the law to stop therapy and that our son could be taken into custody of another family. We signed a paper that released the hospital from responsibility since Jo insisted that he was healed. Our local social officer in Perth-Andover told me that it was the law, but he would take no legal action.

A month later we three started deputation in Ontario. There we received notice that the St. John oncologist had taken action and we were to appear in court the next day. We were 1,400 miles away. We arranged for our lawyer to represent us in court, and we would do whatever they desired.

A week later we arrived in Oshawa, Ontario. Brother Barrett Church, an old friend since Bible school days who was having his own battle with cancer, invited us to stay in the church apartment and seek medical help at the Sick Children's Hospital in Toronto.

The new oncologist said he would not force treatment but that the cancer had spread to Jo's chest. Chances for survival were now only five percent. Jo agreed to go on with an experimental treatment, which was much more vigorous and debilitating. Soon his heart could no longer take the treatment and chemotherapy was stopped.

One morning Jo awoke and said, "Mom, I had a dream last night, but I don't know if I should tell you. You may feel sad."

I responded, "Please tell me."

He said he dreamed he was kneeling down and kissing streets of gold. I said, "Just because you have a dream about heaven does not mean you are going to die."

I read passages of Scripture about faith to him every day. He repeated them with me. He had me make signs of faith verses around his room. He invited anyone who visited him first to pray. Jo said, "Maybe I have to suffer so that someday I can go to a faraway country like Russia or Germany as a missionary and suffer for Jesus."

We prayed as never before. Visitors prayed. The Bible school in Oshawa fasted and prayed. Pastors called long distance and prayed for Jo over the phone.

More severe bone pain followed. More radiation. More morphine drip to help alleviate the pain. We prayed until we laughed. I had always wanted time to pray all I wanted, but this was a year and a half! Brother DeMerchant was on deputation, but he had told Jo that he would stop when he wanted him. That time had come.

Jo was paralyzed except for his right arm that God had healed. He could still hold a glass and write! Jo's faith amazed the doctors. Jo had received the Holy Spirit when he was eight years old and was baptized in Jesus' name soon after. He had quite a knowledge of the Bible, as we had ordered many preaching tapes for him. He repeated, "For I reckon that the sufferings of this present time are not worthy to be compared with the glory which shall be revealed in us" (Romans 8:18). Jo asked the doctor how much more time he had.

The oncologist said, "Next year you won't be here."

Jo said, "But I have God."

In the hall the doctor told me that Jo was dying.

I asked Jo to pray after me, "Lord, I belong to You. My life is in Your hands. Do whatever Your will is with my life." He repeated, but every day he expected a miracle that would make him perfectly whole.

On Sunday he asked me to read a book on the Lord's Prayer. I read a chapter that explained how to make out a check and ask for a specific thing. Jo asked me to make out a check. I put June 14, 1992, complete healing for Bennie Jo, from head to toe, and that he wanted to leave the hospital that week. Jo could hardly open his mouth to speak.

Early the next morning Jo shouted, "Dad, I'm healed from head to toe!" His dad was sleeping in the bed beside him and said, "If that is so, raise your hands and thank God!"

Jo responded, "Oh no, Dad, I am still in the hospital. I can only raise my right hand." We can only believe that Jo was dying and saw his perfect, celestial body he was ready to enter.

"For we know that, if our earthly house of this tabernacle were dissolved, we have a building of God, a house not made with hands, eternal in the heavens" (II Corinthians 5:1). Jo's vision helped me to understand that when we leave this earthly body we have the promise of a celestial one.

It was Monday, June 15, 1992. Brother DeMerchant buzzed me in my room. I came running about four blocks. I felt as if angels were whispering in my ears. I was thanking the Lord. Something wonderful had happened. I came to Jo's room. My husband stepped out. He said Jo was speaking in tongues, and then he was gone. I could feel no sadness. I stepped in, and Jo's eyes were looking up towards heaven. I closed them and thanked the Lord again. I knew Jo's eyes had seen God.

My husband said, "The Lord giveth, and the Lord taketh away." He was brokenhearted. All of his dreams for his only son had been shattered. Jo would have been sixteen the following August. God gave me supernatural grace through it all.

My husband was at a loss as to where to start arrangements. The phone rang in the hospital room. It was Brother Wayne Rooks. He said he had tried all over to find us early that morning. "What's up, friend?" he inquired. He gave my husband the home phone of Brother Judd and others for immediate help. How good our God is! Our cousins, the Melvin DeMerchants, came quickly to help us move out of our room at the hospital in Toronto. Our friends in Oshawa helped us to move out of the church apartment the same day. Our daughter, Pamela, arrived from college in St. Paul, and we drove twelve hours the next day to Perth-Andover, where friends and relatives helped us. Thank God for the church!

We were able to return to Brazil in August 1992 for our sixth term. Jo had told me to tell Dad there would be a great revival in Brazil. We are believing to that end.

••

After graduating from Apostolic Bible Institute, Bennie DeMerchant and his wife, Theresa, ministered briefly in the Atlantic District before receiving their missionary appointment to the Amazon basin of Brazil in 1964. Brother DeMerchant is the field superintendent of Brazil. The DeMerchants live and work out of Manaus, Amazonas, where Sister DeMerchant directs three Bible schools with approximately 150 students. The new Manaus District Bible school complex will accommodate 300 students.

Chapter 18

Protected by Angels

by **Stuart Lassetter**, Ecuador

Bermudez Cabrera, an Ecuadorian minister, was sent to pastor in a small, rural community of just a few buildings. He worked diligently among the humble folk that live on small farms in the hill country in the province of Loja. God began to bless this man's ministry and people began to repent. They were baptized in Jesus' name, and God filled them with the Holy Ghost.

One woman who came to the Lord was totally changed by her experience, but her husband did not like what was going on. He was very antagonistic towards her and irate toward Brother Cabrera. This man came to hate the minister and resolved to kill him, thereby solving the "problem."

In this small community, everyone was aware of the situation and knew of the death threat against Brother Cabrera. The rumor said that on a certain Sunday night after the church service was over, the assassination would take place. The irate husband was on the back row during the service, and everyone knew that he had a pistol with him. The service began and then concluded with an altar call. Soon after that, when the visiting and fellowship had ended, the saints drifted away to their homes and the man also disappeared. Brother Cabrera put the padlock on the church door and began to walk down the lane to his little shack of a home.

As he walked along, his mind was on the Lord Jesus and all of His blessings. Brother Cabrera was thinking how wonderful it was to be filled with the Holy Ghost and to know Jesus personally. He was getting in the frame of mind to die and meet the Lord, for he knew that the threat was serious and that the man intended to kill him. No police or soldiers were anywhere near the remote area to offer protection. Brother Cabrera's mind was on the Lord as he walked along, thinking each step would be his last.

Before too long, however, he arrived at his door and no harm had come. He did not understand why nothing had happened. Nevertheless, he rejoiced, prayed for a while, and then went to sleep.

A few days later, Brother Cabrera met this would-be assassin and mustered the courage to strike up a conversation with him. He admitted that he knew the man was upset with his wife's experience with God and understood that the man had decided to kill him. Brother Cabrera asked why nothing had happened.

The man replied that yes, he had intended to kill Brother Cabrera after church that Sunday night and had waited in ambush along the path from the church to Brother Cabrera's house. But the man said, "As you came around the curve to where I was waiting, I saw you were surrounded with a circle of soldiers, each one in uniform and with a gun. I thought, I'm outgunned tonight with only a pistol against machine guns. I'll wait until another time."

Although Brother Cabrera did not see these angels, they appeared as Ecuadorian soldiers to the would-be killer. They protected God's man as the Lord has done down through the centuries.

Another time did not come for the assassin. Only a short time later, this man who had risen up against God's anointed minister became drunk at a party on the second floor of a building and fell out of the window. He died as a result of the fall.

••

Stuart Lassetter, a former associate professor at Eastern Kentucky University, and his wife, Nancy, received their appointment to Colombia in May 1981. During their first term, Brother Lassetter helped to establish the Bible school and construct its facilities, taught, trained, and preached. Sister Lassetter also taught in the Bible school.

The Lassetters transferred to Ecuador in 1986. Brother Lassetter, the field superintendent and president of the Bible school, teaches pastoral studies, devotes much time to leadership training, and is involved in various administrative activities. Sister Lassetter works with pastors' wives and women leaders in leadership training.

Chapter 19

Juana Garcia of Caracas

by **James Burton**, Uruguay

In 1958 Venezuela elected its first democratic president, Romulo Betancourt. I remember reading an article in the *Reader's Digest* in 1961. The article said that President Betancourt would never finish his five-year term. The Communist Party was growing fast and was determined that they would rule Venezuela. The writer of the article fully expect him to be overthrown.

We arrived in Venezuela in June 1962, during Betancourt's democratic rule. The communists were still sure of victory that never came. Uprisings and political upheavals greeted us. We were in constant danger as we traveled.

Caracas, the capital of Venezuela, was a city of about a million people in 1962. One of our first little churches was founded in Caracas in May 1962, a month before we arrived.

In August I decided to visit them. I went by bus from the city of San Cristobal to Caracas, about a twelve-hour, precarious trip. We arrived in the city in an atmosphere of tension. I immediately took a taxi to the barrio called Charneca, where our newly founded church was located. The taxi driver quickly got my suitcase out and then drove off like light-

How Do You Tell a Hungry Soul She Cannot Have a Bible?

ning! I would have liked to have jumped in and left with him, as shots rang out on the mountainside. But, alas, it was too late. He was gone.

I looked up at the barrio. All the houses were dangling on the side of the mountain. The government soldiers were fighting in this barrio against the communist takeover. At that time everyone said it was in vain, for the barrio did not want a democratic government.

I prayed as I began to climb the mountainside. One of the sisters had moved from another city to Caracas. She saw me coming up the mountainside and ran down to greet me. She wrenched the suitcase out of my hand and threw it up on her head. (In those days that was the way it was done; everything was carried on their heads.) Together we started up the mountainside.

From time to time shots could be heard. Someone from behind threw a rock at me. It was probably meant for my head, but it hit my left shoulder. Oh, how it hurt, but I did not dare to turn around and look.

At last, near the top, I saw a three-story house precariously perched on the side. Three stories? It was actually three rooms, one on top of the other. As there was no space to build out, it had to be built up. There were three rooms, and each room was the living space for a family. Our pastor lived on the third floor—in his one room that also served as our church.

We climbed the outside steps and were greeted by the pastor and his family. Then I set up my cot in a corner of the room. There is where I slept during the next four nights.

Slept? That was almost a joke, as all night long the soldiers and communists shot at each other. During the church services we had to fall to the floor several times. I remember in one of the church services the shooting was so bad that I stuck my head in the pulpit. Bullets were flying through the room. And though they were not shooting at us, bullets have no eyes nor are they respecters of persons.

Years later I told this experience while on furlough. One dear brother came up to me after the service and asked, "Why did you put your head in the pulpit? Don't you know that you do not have to worry until the one with your name comes along?" This surprised me and without thinking I answered him, "I am not worried about the bullet with my name on it but the one that says, 'To whom it may concern.'" He just looked at me and walked off.

Present in the four-day revival was the pastor, his family, and the four other people who were already baptized in Jesus' name. They did not miss a night. We almost always had five or six visitors. We had four great services.

One night I had just gotten up from praying when a very hard-looking, tough, sad woman came through the door. She sat down and looked around. The others would not make eye contact with her. The pastor, who was sitting next to me, would not look up. The whole atmosphere changed to one of fear. I asked the pastor who she was. Without looking up, he replied, "Pray, brother, pray. She is the communist chief of this barrio. She will stop at nothing until everyone in the barrio lines up with her Communist Party. She feels that her party is the answer to all the problems of Venezuela."

I looked at the pastor and said, "Isn't this great! I get to tell her about a more perfect way." I could see that he was not sure if he agreed with me. Oh yes, he was in agreement about the message, but I am sure he doubted if it would do any good to tell her about it.

He told me that her name was Juana Garcia. During the singing, specials, testimonies, and prayer, she spent her time looking around. If she made eye contact with anyone, she would snarl and mock him or her. You can imagine what effect this had on the small congregation. Everyone was terrified. I was determined with the help of the Lord that I was not going to let her affect me.

It was time for the preaching. I asked the Lord to give me wisdom when I preached and to give me, in Jesus' name, this woman for Him.

How Do You Tell a Hungry Soul She Cannot Have a Bible?

When I entered the pulpit, she looked straight at me. Defiance was in her eyes. She was the leader in the barrio, and all must be subject to her. But by the end of the message, her countenance had changed. Before anyone could realize what was happening, Juana was in the altar, crying and sobbing. Between sobs, she was saying, "Oh, Jesus, Jesus! This is what I have been looking for!" She would say this over and over again. At last she said it no more; the Lord took control of her tongue and she began to speak in other tongues. How we all rejoiced with her.

At the end of four days, the pastor baptized four more people in Jesus' name. Sister Juana was one of them. Who was the first to step into the water? Sister Juana. She was a natural-born leader and was always that way.

Is that the end of the story? No, not by any means. Sister Juana told me that she had much to do and to rectify. She said, "This is what the world needs, not communism." She undid all that she had done in favor of communism in the barrio. Many of her former communist friends came to the Lord. Everyone respected her for her complete about-face.

Under her personal soulwinning, Barrio Charneca was a model barrio within a year. No soldiers walked the streets. No shots rang out. The government knew it had been turned around—not by soldiers, not by bullets, but by a woman filled with the power of the Holy Spirit. She practiced the gospel.

Sister Juana seldom came to church without a visitor. She was always bright and cheery. I can say without exaggeration that through her, directly and indirectly, hundreds of people have been saved from the ruination of sin. Her granddaughter whom she raised when she came to the Lord has never wavered. Juana's great-grandchildren, who are now teenagers, are great examples to the other young people.

She worked for the Lord fifteen years. I was not with her when she died. However, those who were told me that she raised her feeble hands to heaven and gave thanks that she had been privileged to know the truth. Then she began to speak in tongues and went on to her eternal reward.

Caracas now has fifteen United Pentecostal churches. The church that Juana was saved in is going on. It is not the central church, but its membership is nearing four hundred people.

Around the world there are other unknown Sister Juanas. I give thanks for each and every one of them, especially for Sister Juana Garcia.

••

James and Martha Burton are the senior missionaries of the United Pentecostal Church. They have been under continuous appointment since 1961. Under his leadership the UPC of Venezuela grew to a large and stable force of over 60,000 constituents. In recognition of his impact on the nation, Venezuelan President Carlos Andres Perez conferred upon Brother Burton the Orden Al Merito En El Trabajo, the second highest award given in Venezuela for outstanding achievement.

In September 1990 the General Board of the UPCI appointed Brother Burton as the regional director of South America. In this position, he oversaw the ministry of the UPCI throughout South America until his resignation in 1996. Although Brother and Sister Burton had planned to retire, they instead asked permission to revive the Uruguayan church. They arrived in Montevideo in early 1997.

Chapter 20

Flying High on Deputation

by **Bennie Blunt**, Tonga/Western Samoa

While traveling in a certain part of the country where hotel prices were very expensive, we gladly accepted the pastor's offer to stay at the church. He and his wife had a small apartment in the church. He explained that the only thing they had available for us to sleep on was a queen-size air mattress. He assured us, however, that it was quite comfortable, and we agreed to take him up on his offer. The catch was that the only place they had to put it for us to have privacy was on the platform behind the pulpit. This arrangement proved so comfortable that we spent two nights with them. We then went on our way to another service.

Later that week, we need to travel to a special dedication service to the south of them, and this pastor and his wife expressed a desire to accompany us. That afternoon as we arrived he said, "There's no need for you to drive that long distance back to the north, so why don't you all just spend the night with us?" So, he began to air up the mattress. I noticed that one end of it was little misshapen.

We went on to the service and arrived back at the church about 1:30 AM, totally exhausted, and fell into the bed. About 3:30 AM we were abruptly awakened by a series of loud pops similar to a string of firecrackers exploding. This was due to the straps inside the air mattress giving away. This caused a big bubble to form at the foot of the mattress.

I suggested to my wife that we let a small amount of air out, hoping to improve the situation. Upon lying back down, we quickly discovered that was the wrong thing to do. The good part was now flat, and all of the air was in the bubble at the foot. I said, "This is not going to work! We are going to have to get up!" At that suggestion, she just rolled off onto the floor.

This allowed the foot of the mattress to shoot straight into the air. My feet were sticking almost straight up; my head was on the floor. Laughing, my wife asked, "Are you all right?"

I answered, "If I ever get down from here, I'll be okay!" Flipping over, I managed to extract myself. Nothing compares to hanging upside down, like a bat, behind the pulpit in a darkened sanctuary. We both had a good laugh and spent the rest of the night on the hard, hard floor.

We moved on to the next city, where the pastor placed us in the Hilton Hotel. I can say with the apostle Paul, "I know both how to be abased, and I know how to abound." But, through it all, we are thankful for every kindness that has been shown to us.

•••

Brother and Sister Blunt received their October 1989 appointment as UPCI missionaries in October 1989. They arrived in Fiji in September 1992, where they taught in the Bible school while he also pastored the Bible school church.

In December 1994 Brother and Sister Blunt transferred to Tonga. Brother Blunt is the field superintendent of the Tongan church. They have established and teach in the United Pentecostal Bible College in Tonga. Brother Blunt is also the area coordinator for American Samoa, Western Samoa, and the Cook Islands.

Chapter 21

Recapping the Rash Story in Missions

by Carol Rash

Brother Daryl Rash and I had felt a burden for missions ever since we were very young but were not called to a particular field until we attended the general conference in Salt Lake City in 1973. The foreign missions service on Sunday was one of the most outstanding services we had ever attended. During that service God called Brother Rash to the country of Indonesia as Brother and Sister George White stood on the platform, crying because they were not appointed to return to the land of their calling. Tongues and interpretation came forth, and God said, "Is there not a man who can take the place of the man in the white hair?" From that day forward we began praying about going to Indonesia, and we received our appointment at the next year's general conference.

In 1975 we left beautiful California with our four children to go to the land of our calling. We could not begin to tell all the marvelous things that happened in the next four years as we learned a new language and learned to love the people and culture of Indonesia. We saw many people filled with the Holy Ghost as well as many healed in soul and body. Along with the wonderful times, we saw God bring us through many serious illnesses such as malaria, amoebae, dengue fever, and, yes, even days of depression.

One of the greatest miracles is being able to live four years in such a country without being killed in a traffic accident. There are laws for the road, but people do not know what they are. And they do not pay attention to the ones they know. At least twice, trucks came so close to us as they passed that they hit our side-view mirror, sending shattered glass through the opened windows. (We did not have air conditioning.)

One day Brother Rash was attending a conference on the island of Sulawesi and was being peddled downhill in a becak [bicycle taxi] along with Brother Kewengian, the national superintendent. As they entered a very busy intersection, the driver could not stop the becak and they could see that were going to hit a pickup truck. Brother Rash only had time to call out "JESUS!" as they caught the truck's rear bumper, completely pulling it off while the little becak did not even budge. Oh how we thank the Lord for the many times He was there to protect us!

Indonesia was our first love and calling, and we thought we would spend the rest of our lives there. When furlough time came, we packed all of our belongings in fourteen barrels and put them in the garage of a missionary in Medan, Sumatra, who was with another group. While we were home, our visas and those of the other United Pentecostal Church missionaries who were serving in Indonesia were canceled. We could not even go back to obtain our things. We tried to go to Malaysia, but that too was a closed country.

We heard of the need for a missionary in Vienna, Austria, and accepted the challenge. We arrived there in 1980 with our two youngest children. Our two older children, Jonathan and Becky, remained in the United States since they had finished high school. We entered into intensive study of the German language and pastored a small congregation that had recently been started by another missionary. The Lord really blessed the work. By the end of the year, we needed a new building because of the growth of the group.

This work and country were so totally different from Indonesia that it was as though God had taken us out of the oven and put us into a freezer—in more ways than one. We had moved from the hot tropics of living on the equator to the northern, cold climate of Europe. But the warm fires of the Holy Ghost were burning in our little church and in the lives of each new one who found new life in Christ. His love can keep us warm no matter where we are!

After our year in Austria, the former missionary planned to return to the work. Brother Harry Scism, the general director of Foreign Missions, asked us to go to Holland to replace Brother and Sister George Craft as they left for furlough. This meant yet another country and language for the Rash family.

Again we accepted the challenge and were so glad we did. We really loved the Dutch people and their country. The green fields and pastures, fenced in only by water canals, were so beautiful. The Lord added to the church such as should be saved, and it was a year of revival for the little church in Dordrecht. We found that though the German and Dutch languages are similar in some ways, they are very different. We had to program our minds completely to this new language. The whole year was a year of healing for our family emotionally and in every way.

At the end of that year, we were asked if we would go to Wiesbaden, Germany, to serve again as furlough replacements. Since we had already studied German, we accepted that challenge too. We pastored the American military church and also the German congregation in Wiesbaden until we left on furlough a year later. We grew to love the people and saw a mighty move of God among the Germans.

Later we back to Wiesbaden for another term, but this time without our children. During this term we went through some extremely difficult times in the work. God, however, proved Himself to be so real and powerful and brought us through with victory. From that group in the military church

How Do You Tell a Hungry Soul She Cannot Have a Bible?

we now have three United Pentecostal preachers serving in various places around the world. We are particularly excited about Brother and Sister Rufus Parker, who are now pastoring the church in Okinawa, Japan, and assisting Brother Paul Dennis with the Asian military district. To God be the glory for the things He has done!

Brother Rash is now an associate pastor and missions director at Christian Life Center in Stockton, California. (With God's help, the church was number one in missions giving for the United Pentecostal Church International for 1996-97.)

We also teach and work in the Bible college and are trying to place the burden for missions into the lives of young people who can carry on where we left off. We say to them, "As the Father hath sent me, so send I you." We have sent several young couples from Stockton to the mission field as Associates In Missions. One of them, Brian and Esther Henry, were appointed as missionaries to Papua New Guinea. We are so proud of them!

We are so thankful for all God has done and will do until the day He calls us all home to be forever by His side. Missions is still the heartbeat of God!

• •

Daryl and Carol Rash left the home missions church they pioneered in Grass Valley, California, to go to Indonesia. Their submission to the will of God later led them from the tropics to the snows of northern and central Europe. One of their coworkers stated, "They have revival wherever they go." Even when they returned to Stockton, California, and joined the faculty of Christian Life College, they continued to experience the thrill of revival as Brother Rash pastored the Asian congregation.

Today the Rashes still retain their love and burden for missions. However, instead of going themselves, they are helping to prepare others to go. May their spirit of submission and sacrifice be deeply rooted in the hearts of their students.

124

Chapter 22

Laborers Together with God

by **J. S. Leaman**, Director of Promotion

"For we are labourers together with God: ye are God's husbandry, ye are God's building" (I Corinthians 3:9).

In 1969 the Foreign Missions Division of the UPCI introduced the Faith Promise plan of giving. Faith Promise is asking the Lord about giving to the cause of reaching the lost world. We ask the Lord what He wants to channel through us each month toward the support of sending missionaries to preach the gospel to the lost. We become laborers together with God in our giving.

Two verses in Proverbs help us understand how Faith Promise works: "Trust in the LORD with all thine heart; and lean not unto thine own understanding. In all thy ways acknowledge him, and he shall direct thy paths" (Proverbs 3:5-6).

As we ask the Lord, we may be surprised as to what He may impress us to give on a monthly basis. We may doubt our ability to do what He impresses us to do. But let us consider the Scripture: "Now unto him that is able to do exceedingly abundantly above all that we ask or think, according to the power that worketh in us" (Ephesians 3:20).

A number of years ago I was in a church for a weekend

How Do You Tell a Hungry Soul She Cannot Have a Bible?

missionary conference. The pastor received the Faith Promise commitments at the close of the Sunday night service. A widow came up all excited at what had happened to her in the service and related the following story.

She said, first of all, she had no income. Then she explained that her husband had died some years earlier and he had not paid enough money into Social Security for her to have any pension. She went on to explain that she had felt to make a ten-dollar monthly commitment. I knew that was a step of faith since she had no income.

She filled out her Faith Promise commitment card for ten dollars and turned it in. At the close of the service, the church gathered around the altar and prayed. When she walked back to her seat, she opened her purse and found a hundred-dollar bill. She related excitedly, "I do not know where it came from!" However, she had ten months' worth of her year's commitment before she walked out of church that night.

The next morning one of the men in the church took me to the airport to catch my flight. On the way I told him about the widow's experience the night before. He got excited as he explained that he knew who had put the money in the widow's purse. He said that after the choir sang, his wife came to him and said she felt she should give the widow some money. At the time he did not know how much she had given her. He exclaimed, "You've made my day!" because the Lord had used his wife meet the widow's need.

Another widow in Ohio felt the Lord direct her to make a Faith Promise commitment of fifty dollars a month. Within the month she received a letter from her son. He said, "Mom, I feel I am to start sending you fifty dollars a month." She was surprised as she said that had never happened before.

On a Wednesday night in Illinois, a ten-year-old boy had an exciting experience in his church's missionary Faith Promise service. He had asked the Lord what he should commit and felt impressed to commit four dollars a month.

It was a big step of faith for him, as he did not know where it would come from. A few days later he received a check for forty-eight dollars from an insurance company as a result of an accident his mother had had a couple of years before. He had been with her in the car accident, and for some unknown reason the insurance company paid him forty-eight dollars. He was elated at how the Lord had provided his year's Faith Promise money.

A couple in Tennessee was struggling financially. She had been laid off work for quite some time from the telephone company. Nevertheless, they felt the Lord speak to them about their commitment. They made their Faith Promise definitely by faith. The next morning she was called back to work. She called her husband to tell him the good news. However, his line was busy. He was trying to call her to report that he had received a raise that morning.

One thing to keep in mind is that where God guides, He provides. It is His will that we labor with Him in our giving. If we will become channels for His blessings, He will supply as we give.

Why not give the Lord a chance to bless you with your finances as you give so that the gospel of Jesus Christ can be taken to a world that is desiring the message of truth?

A few years ago I walked into a church for a missions conference and saw a banner across the front of the church. It read:

> Some give by going;
> Some go by giving.
> Without both
> There is no missions.

If you cannot go in person, why not go in purse?

Following his graduation from Crooksville (Ohio) High School, John S. Leaman attended Apostolic Bible Institute in St. Paul, Minnesota, where he met his future wife. On September 28, 1957 he married Shirley Hall in University City, Missouri.

After graduating from ABI, the Leamans moved to Lancaster, Ohio, and assisted Pastor R. G. Cook for seven years. During this time they rejoiced in the births of Rodney and Melanie. In June 1965, the Leaman family moved to Wausau, Wisconsin, to begin a home missions work. Their home missions work grew, and Brother Leaman served the Wisconsin District as its youth president from 1968 to 1971.

In November 1970 Brother Leaman returned to Lancaster to be R. G. Cook's associate pastor at First Apostolic Church. The church elected Brother Leaman its pastor in 1973. During his tenure as pastor, the church was consistently among the top twenty churches in giving to foreign missions. From 1971 to 1976 he also served as the Ohio District youth president.

In November 1975 the Foreign Missions Board asked Brother Leaman to serve as Foreign Missions Division's director of promotion. For the next fifteen years, promoting Faith Promise consumed his weekends while the weekdays found him attending to the general affairs of foreign missions. During these years he made several trips to visit the missionaries on location.

At the 1990 General Conference in New Orleans, Brother Leaman assumed the responsibility of the director of education and Associates In Missions (AIM). Under his leadership the AIM program continued to grow while the overseas Bible school maintained a high standard of training.

In September 1994 the FMB asked Brother Leaman to return to his former position as director of promotion. Brother Leaman continues to hold Faith Promise services on the weekends. During the week he again schedules the missionaries' deputational travel, communicates with district foreign missions directors, oversees the publication of promotional materials, and plans for the upcoming general conference.